The First Pancake

Bon Appetit !!
xo
Joey

The First Pancake

A Recipe for Delectable Life Transitions

Tory G. Wilcox

iUniverse, Inc.
New York Bloomington

The First Pancake
A Recipe for Delectable Life Transitions

iUniverse books may be ordered through booksellers or by contacting:

iUniverse
1663 Liberty Drive
Bloomington, IN 47403
www.iuniverse.com
1-800-Authors (1-800-288-4677)

ISBN: 978-0-595-46836-2 (pbk)
ISBN: 978-0-595-62599-4 (cloth)
ISBN: 978-0-595-91127-1 (ebk)

Printed in the United States of America

iUniverse rev. date: 11/26/2008

Dedication

This book is dedicated to the ones I love, Gray and
Reid, my most precious pancakes.

"We know what we are but not what we can be."

—William Shakespeare, *Hamlet*

Ingredients

Monologue

Okay, so who am I, and why in the world am I making pancakes for you? I thought that you would never ask! As you might have noticed on the front cover, my name is Tory Wilcox, a life transition expert seasoned by years of academic and experiential training. I am a veteran of numerous transitions, including a professional metamorphosis from a financial services executive to a psychotherapist and coach, a personal adjustment to a nasty chronic pain affliction and a divorce. My education and experience have empowered me to make my perfect pancake, at least for this phase of my life.

In the chapters that follow, I intend to equip you with the best available utensils to prepare your own prettiest pancakes by following my recipe for delectable life transitions. I have been fortunate enough to help my clients, colleagues, and counterparts in the worlds of business, psychology, and beyond to survive transitions and attain superior satisfaction with their lives. I hope that you will allow me the same privilege by reading on as I share my experience and my ingredients for successful life transitions.

The First Pancake Phenomenon

"The first pancake is always spoiled."
—English adage

Have you ever had the "first pancake experience"? You painstakingly follow the instructions on the package: heat the griddle or skillet to the recommended temperature, blend and stir the required ingredients, beat out the lumps, pour the batter into the pan, wait for the ideal number of those tiny bubbles to form, and then flip. Voilà, the first pancake—only it is not golden brown and cooked to perfection as you had anticipated. It is bronzed in the center and around the perimeter but not throughout; it can't hold a candle to Aunt Jemima's, which is pictured on the box's cover, so you feed the imperfect disk to your dog, your goldfish, your unsuspecting infant, or your garbage disposal.

Now it's time for pancake number two. You follow precisely the same steps, only this time after the flip, there it is—round, golden, and suitable to serve to your partner without the fear of facial expressions that obviate the need for words. Why does the first pancake turn out not quite right if and when you follow the same procedures for the whole stack? And why settle for the first pancake when superior, more satisfying ones are readily available?

Based on my expertise, I can safely say that undergoing adult life transitions is much like making a stack of pancakes. The process begins with a wake-up call, be it internally or externally initiated. This alarm alerts us to examine the first pancake we have made, for example, our college selection, our career choice,

1

our partner, or our lifestyle. If that first pancake is not fulfilling, I want to empower you to pitch it and prepare better pancakes for your own enjoyment. At first, you will feel as though you have been tossed into a blender, as if your world is falling apart. There is no question that transition times can be uncomfortable or even painful. I believe that the phrases "no pain, no gain" and "no guts, no glory" were coined for life transitions. Equipped with the right tools, however, you can not only get through the blender of emotions that a transition will evoke but you can emerge a happier individual who devours more perfect pancakes in the form of superior satisfaction with your life. Once you digest the changes you have made and the transition process you have been through, you should feel confident about making better pancakes and enjoying the rewards. Then, you will want to keep adding to the stack during your adult life and make every pancake the very best that you can.

Transition Times

> "Life is pleasant. Death is peaceful. It's
> the transition that's troublesome."
> —Isaac Asimov

Transition psychology originated in the 1960s with work on bereavement, family crises, and depression by theorists like Elisabeth Kübler-Ross. Although psychologists initially researched transitions when coping with trauma and loss, both positive (e.g., marriage) and negative (e.g., divorce) events can precipitate psychological disruption and transition. In the 1970s, life span theorists like Daniel Levinson recognized transition as a cause of stress and incorporated transition theory into their life role, life stage, and life span development theories. Accordingly, they developed models of transition to demonstrate how individuals respond to change resulting from significant life events that change the individual's role or environment and, thus, necessitate restructuring of one's self-concept and worldview.

Actually, transition models, like transition itself, go way back. For example, an early transition model can be found in the New Testament, which portrays a movement through conviction/ confession, repentance, and new birth. There are many different models of transition that have merit; for example, Sabina Spencer and John Adams's model of adult transitions, which strikes an experiential chord with me. Their model presents seven stages of transition: immobilization, minimization, self-doubt, letting go, testing out, search for meaning, and internalization. These sound a lot like Kübler-Ross's model for grief stages: denial, anger, bargaining, depression, and acceptance. The similarity of the grief and transition models makes sense because transition always involves a loss or an ending of some sort. These transition (or grief) phases are related to moods and take place over time. The amount of time that an individual takes to cycle through the stages is not fixed and can vary from days to years, depending on the circumstances surrounding the transition and the psychological makeup of the person.

In keeping with the title of this book, I offer you an alternative transition model, which has five stages: t*he wake-up call, the first pancake, the blender, the perfect pancake,* and *digestion.* As we go through each stage, I hope that the pancake framework will provide you with the solace that what you are experiencing during transition times is unsettling but perfectly natural. In fact, you can view transition in a more positive light simply by altering your point of view. For example, would you rather experience a *crisis* or a *crescendo?* An *upheaval* or an *uplifting?* A *change* or a *chance?* I encourage you to reframe the way that you interpret the event by seeing the transition as an opportunity, a new beginning, rather than the end of the world as you know it. Different interpretations of the same event can drastically affect your emotional well-being. If you shift your way of thinking, you change the way you feel, and that is an important skill as you travel through transition times. The one-, three-, five, -seven,- hike stage transition models (including mine) share a common goal, to provide you with the comfort that comes from knowing what to expect during transition times. I simply choose five stages, because seven isn't my lucky number and also is overused in less creative self-help books. Besides, those of us fortunate enough to have all of our digits can count the stages of the pancake model on one hand, and those of us seasoned enough to have weathered numerous transitions have the cognitive faculties to remember five steps, while seven might be pushing our luck.

Frederic Hudson, in his book *The Handbook of Coaching,* distinguishes mini-transitions from life transitions. Mini-transitions renew the lifestyle of an individual, while a life transition transforms the person. A job change within the same company or an industry, the acquisition of new skills, or a relocation is an example of a mini-transition. Marriage, divorce, a complete career change, or a significant deterioration in health or wealth represents a life transition. A life transition involves the loss of something previously experienced, usually leading to introspection and then a transformation of some sort.

> **"Any transition serious enough to alter your definition of self will require not just small adjustments in your way of living and thinking but a full-on metamorphosis."**
> —Martha Beck

Neither type of transition is better or worse than the other; one may simply be more suitable based on an individual's level of happiness in a given phase of life when coupled with external circumstances, challenges, and opportunities. *The First Pancake's* focus is on life transitions rather than changes of a lesser scale; it addresses how to survive your transition successfully, though not always smoothly. I hope, however, that you will find the utensils useful in all of your transitions, large or small. My personal and professional experience with life transitions, as a financial services manager as well as psychotherapist and coach, supports these recommendations. The suggestions are illustrated through my stories and those of others whom I have known professionally and personally.

Recipe: Transition Stages

1. The Wake-up Call
2. The First Pancake
3. The Blender
4. The Perfect Pancake
5. Digestion

The Wake-Up Call

"We must wake ourselves up! Or somebody
else will take our place, and bear our cross,
and thereby rob us of our crown."
—William Booth

How does the first pancake process begin? Typically, it starts with a wake-up call that your actions or someone else's can instigate. After all, you can't prepare pancakes until you wake up with or without a musical, telephonic, or sunrise alarm, and get out of bed. In my case, coffee also is a must before, during, and after preparing pancakes.

For some, an external event, like the birth of a child, the death of a spouse, the loss of a job, the departure of a child for college, a major relocation, or a natural disaster, precipitates a life transition. In other words, someone or something else outside yourself forces you to examine that first pancake. That's what it took for me to wake up and smell the coffee when I lost the job I had held for nineteen years and then, five days later, my mother died. External life-altering events often trigger shock, particularly when they're unforeseen or involuntary. Shock, in turn, triggers a mixture of emotions. Seen in the proper light, however, such events are opportunities to begin a new and improved life chapter. These precipitants represent endings but also beginnings—chances to start over, grow, and transform. Both negative and positive life events can close doors but also open windows of opportunity for growth and development.

Here are some examples from my client and colleague base.

- Jim's wake-up call sadly was the diagnosis of colon cancer that his doctor discovered during a routine baseline colonoscopy. Faced with the prospect of his life being shorter than he expected, he began to rethink his priorities.
- Trudy's children revealed that their nanny had been watching *The Jerry Springer Show* after their afternoon naps and leaving them unattended while she went outside to smoke cigarettes. The image of her children in this situation haunted Trudy and made her reflect on her values.
- Rob's wake-up call was getting fired from his insurance company job of twenty-four years six years before he had hoped to retire and six days before his planned vacation. What did he do?
- Mark just got a new boss who is female, ten years his junior, and highly critical of his every move. His stomach is in a constant knot, and he is getting to work later and later every day. Is this job really worth it, or should Mark tell her to shove it?
- Alex has just graduated from college and moved to Manhattan. She is going to start in an investment bank training program and finds herself feeling excited, scared, and uncertain depending on the day of the week.

You get the picture. The wake-up call signals the reality that you are about to examine that first pancake and undergo a life transition. You may feel like rolling over or hiding under the covers, but if you can talk yourself out of bed and into the kitchen, you will not only survive but learn to make tastier pancakes to enjoy.

The First Pancake

So how do you know when the first pancake has to go? In a culinary context, it's pretty plain. For example, your first pancake looks more like a tortilla or a crêpe. Or perhaps it is overcooked, undercooked, or just plain half-baked. In real life, it can be a little more complicated but not when you are equipped with the proper utensils.

As noted above, we can toss the imperfect disk after an external impetus. Alternatively, the cake can become toast of our own volition. Sometimes, the need for change is painfully obvious. You no longer spring out of bed in the morning, well rested and ready to conquer the day. In fact, you dread the rousing shower, panty hose, commute, and stress—or the shaving, annoying boss, claustrophobic cubicle, and necktie. It is a little-known fact that men actually die sooner than women do because their neckties slowly strangle them. Women are more fortunate because only their legs are suffocated by wearing pantyhose for a prolonged period of time. You may be thinking that whoever invented ties, panty hose, and cubicles was a pretty sick and twisted individual (and I wholeheartedly concur).

In any event, you might be exhausted from restless sleep, interrupted by anxious thoughts or the needs of a child/pet. Your formerly energizing morning workout has become pure drudgery—or even worse—a memory. Perhaps your infant is begging you not to leave, and you cry all of the way to your office. The only good news is that your life is so hectic that you didn't have time to apply mascara, so that your face can't be stained as you weep (even though you know that the child stopped crying the minute you were out of sight and no longer around to manipulate). Been there, done that, got the T-shirt. I don't intend to return there either; in fact, even looking back gives me the creeps.

For others, the chance to transition appears more like an elusive opportunity than a blatant need. You aren't miserable in your current job or lifestyle, but you also aren't fulfilled; you are generally content but not entirely happy. You feel like something is missing but aren't quite sure what it is. Maybe you have never really thought about how you feel as you go through the motions each day on automatic pilot. You basically are out of touch with your feelings, and the pleasure or lack thereof, which you experience while performing certain activities.

People in this gray category might consider pausing long enough at least to take the following Satisfaction with Life Scale, developed by Professor Ed Diener of the University of Illinois (Pavot and Diener, 1993). It is a powerful tool to help us access our feelings.

Satisfaction with Life Scale

Below are five statements with which you may agree or disagree. Using the 1–7 scale below, indicate your level of agreement with each item by placing the appropriate number on the line preceding that item. Please be open and honest in your responses.

- 7 – Strongly agree
- 6 – Agree
- 5 – Slightly agree
- 4 – Neither agree nor disagree
- 3 – Slightly disagree
- 2 – Disagree
- 1 – Strongly disagree

_____ In most ways, my life is close to my ideal.

_____ The conditions of my life are excellent.

_____ I am satisfied with my life.

_____ So far, I have gotten the important things I want in my life.

_____ If I could live my life over, I would change almost nothing.

_____ Total Score (add scores above)

Scoring and Interpretation:

The following interpretations have been adapted to fit the first pancake model.

- 31–35 Extremely satisfied
  For most people in this range, most areas of life like work or school, family, friends, leisure, and personal development are going well. Your current pancake is not perfect, but it is about as good as it gets. People in this category don't have to be complacent. In fact, sometimes highly satisfied people are so because they are constantly growing and developing, searching for a more perfect pancake as they go along.

- 26–30 Satisfied
  Satisfied people believe that their lives are mostly good, that life is more good than bad. They, too, may be growing, developing, and making more pancakes to get to the top of the stack. You can be motivated by the areas of life with which you're dissatisfied and seek out positive change.

- 21–25 Slightly satisfied
  This category represents the average life satisfaction. Do you prefer average pancakes, or most delicious ones? People in this range may have one or two domains of their lives that need large improvement or require minor improvements in all areas to feel more satisfied. In either event, change is required to achieve greater satisfaction, so please get cooking.

- 20 Neutral
  Tasteless, flavorless, bland, blah. I know that you can make better.

- 15–19 Slightly dissatisfied
  People in this range may have small but significant problems in a number of arenas or large problems in one area. Continual dissatisfaction calls for

reflection and change. A small level of dissatisfaction can be motivational, but a large amount can be distracting and lead to dysfunction. It is time to make some better pancakes.

- 10–14 Dissatisfied
  This score indicates substantial dissatisfaction with your life. If this condition originates following a wake-up call (a stressful event), hopefully the dissatisfaction will resolve after the blender. If the condition persists, however, or if dissatisfaction is impairing your functioning, you may need the help of a professional to guide you back into the kitchen.

- 5–9 Extremely dissatisfied
  This suggests extreme unhappiness with your life, often dissatisfaction in multiple areas of your world. If this feeling lingers, change is necessary to restore emotional health and likely requires the help of a friend, family member, professional counselor, coach, or sous chef.

If you prefer to take this survey online, please visit www. authentichappiness.com, a valuable and free Web site developed and maintained by the University of Pennsylvania Positive Psychology Center whose director is Dr. Martin P. Seligman, the founder of positive psychology. Positive psychology is a contemporary and vital branch of the science, supported by research evidencing that positive emotions, character traits, and healthy institutions make you feel more satisfied with life and happier to boot.

Like pancakes, life satisfaction is made from a recipe with a number of ingredients rather than just one critical component. Some of the ingredients are the quality of social relationships; performance at work, school, or another role (like homemaker, grandparent, or caregiver); satisfaction with self; spiritual life; leisure pursuits; and growth and development opportunities. Goals that are congruent with one's values, work that maximizes one's strengths, and solid social support can increase satisfaction. The good news is that there are many ways to increase life satisfaction, and one of the most effective is to seek out continually opportunities to change and grow. This can be uncomfortable, which leads us to our next stage, the blender.

The Blender

"Man has a limited biological capacity for
change. When this capacity is overwhelmed,
the capacity is future shock."
—Alvin Toffler

After you have parted with that first pancake, you most likely
will feel as though you have been tossed into the blender, which
is where you emotionally react to the first pancake stage. Just as
the ingredients for delicious pancakes need to be processed, so
do your emotions. Otherwise, you won't be able to digest, enjoy,
or be satisfied with the end product, your new and revised life.
In the blender, you most likely will cycle through a blend of
emotions, including agony, anger, anxiety, denial, depression,
despair, ecstasy, elation, hope, joy, and sadness. At the beginning
of a transition, the prevailing emotion often is shock. This
shock can occur whether or not the changes are anticipated or
unanticipated, voluntary or involuntary. Typically, the shock is
greatest when the event is unanticipated and involuntary, like
a surprise pink slip in your inbox, an unforeseen divorce, or a
sudden tornado. For example, your spouse comes in the room
and says, "Honey, here's your dry-cleaning, and, oh, the order to
appear at our divorce hearing in the morning," or your boss calls
you into his office and explains, "We're downsizing, and your
position has been eliminated, so please pack up your things this
afternoon."

The dominant mood in this scenario depends on whether the
event was expected (like giving birth or initiating a divorce) or

unexpected (like the loss of a loved one or a natural disaster). The mood swings experienced during this stage can resemble those associated with bipolar disorder but hopefully don't cause the same level of distress or impairment. Speaking of which, the DSM-IV (*Diagnostic and Statistical Manual of Mental Disorders*) used by mental health professionals doesn't really contain a code for transition per se. Adjustment Disorder is made up of emotional and/or behavioral symptoms that come on within three months of a stressor and endure for six months (acute) or longer (chronic). "The essential feature of an Adjustment Disorder is the development of clinically significant emotional or behavioral symptoms in response to an identifiable psychosocial stressor or stressors" (DSM-IV-TR, p. 679). In addition, Other Conditions include bereavement and academic, acculturation, identity, occupational, phase of life, relational, and religious or spiritual problems. These are reactions to life events that cause some level of discomfort but not noticeable impairment. If your transition interferes with your occupational, academic, or social functioning, please seek help from an objective and qualified third party who can facilitate recovery, restore your previous level of functioning, and equip you with the coping tools to weather future storms.

My own most disruptive, yet inspirational transition occurred at age forty-two, when as I previously noted, my nineteen-year stint at a financial institution ended and then, five days later, my mother died. Not to mention, becoming a forty-something woman represents a transition in and of itself. As a sage Home Depot employee told me,

"A woman is old when a man stops looking, and a man is old when he stops looking."

I had led such a charmed life that up until this point, I had never even attended a funeral. I used to joke with my friends that they were lucky to know me because doing so apparently all but assured their immortality. In part because my job was winding down (in other words, it was history), I had the privilege of being present when my mother died at home in her own bed. I recommend this to others if at all possible, because witnessing the end allows you to say good-bye and obtain closure at least regarding the reality of the event.

When my position was eliminated and I left the bank, I found it very bittersweet. On the one hand, I felt a sense of newfound freedom and opportunity. My heart actually raced when I saw my sons, Gray and Reid, emerge from school, and I enjoyed the stories of their days while their reactions were fresh. I got to wait in the car pool line with all of the other mothers who used to take a few steps back when I said that I worked full-time, as though they were afraid that they might catch my dreaded disease.

On the other hand, I was anxious about what the future might hold and sad that I had left a nineteen-year professional stint without so much as a pancake party thrown in my honor. In my case, the loss of my mother, which created a vast void in my support network, naturally aggravated my despair. Neither my professional, nor personal loss was unexpected. My position had been eliminated six months earlier, and I had gotten to spend that era adding virtually nothing to the GNP while turning up my nose at the job offers that had been tendered. Leaving the company was involuntary in the sense that my position had been eliminated but voluntary in the sense that I chose not to stay on in other roles. My mother had been diagnosed with terminal lung cancer eight months earlier, which had provided time to prepare for that blow.

One winter morning, I spent the entire time before school in shrew mode with my sons. "Get up! Get your shoes on! Get ready! Get in the car! Get the stuff you forgot! Get your belts and ties on! Get out of the car! Get going!" On the drive to work, I was thinking about how difficult my lifestyle can be and how stressful and taxing life can become. Once in my office, my first client arrived and told me how anxious she had been feeling. Her food stamps had run out, her teenage son was back in jail, and she continually suffered from horrible nightmares about the night someone had been fatally shot in her home. Working with her to alleviate some of her anxiety somehow lifted my mood as well.

The greatest risk of the blender stage is becoming stuck, overwhelmed, and unable to think or act. Have you ever forgotten to take that metal spoon out before starting the blender and suddenly heard the most awful noise and perhaps even smelled the beginnings of an electrical fire? That would be stuck. It is important to spend long enough in the blender to process the related emotions but not so long as to prevent life from progressing. The DSM-IV doesn't define a "normal" time frame for most Other Conditions. That's a good thing because for bereavement you are supposed to get over it in about two months to be labeled "normal." The transition process usually takes from six to twelve months or longer. Some factors that can facilitate shorter and more successful transitions are good physical health, economic security, emotional well-being, and, last but certainly not least, reading *The First Pancake.* Poor health, economic challenges, and/or emotional insecurity can impede the transition process and result in getting stuck.

One of my psychotherapy clients, Matt, was hit by a drunk driver seven years before I met him. Up to that point, he had worked very hard to rise above a challenging upbringing and obtain a job of which he was proud and which provided economic security. After spending a few months in intensive care, Matt was discharged from the hospital, and he completed physical rehabilitation so that he could walk again with his former gait almost restored. He continued, however, to replay the accident while awake and was unable to sleep; he was unfit to return to work or to let go of the anger about about how the accident had changed his life. Matt's economic security had been jeopardized, and he lacked a good support system. He remained paralyzed for years by his feelings of anger, resentment, and low self-worth. Obviously, the accident was unanticipated and involuntary, and he lacked the resources with which to cope.

Unlike Matt, I had been fortunate to not only be in good health but also receive severance pay because of my tenure. These factors allowed me to revel in an ecstatic mood without immediate despair.

Similarly, another client, Jean, filed for divorce after twenty years in a marriage in which she had been unhappy for some time. An unfamiliar sense of freedom energized her even though her financial security had been compromised. She had a wide network of family and friends on which she could rely for support during her transition to single life and her return to work. Jean hadn't worked since having her son twelve years earlier; however, she had been able to find a job that had fit her skills and experience within six months. She also had begun to run for exercise and competed in local road races. The cardio competitions benefited her physical and emotional health as she began her new life chapter as a happy single working mother.

A final example of how social and spiritual support and positive emotions like optimism can enhance transition. Right on the heels of my losses, a new colleague of mine, Carla, had gone to visit her parents for a well-earned vacation. She had left their house for a half-hour or so to visit her brother. When she returned, she discovered that her sixty-two-year-old mother had collapsed on the living room floor before her powerless husband's eyes and died. Ten months later, Carla's brother committed suicide on the porch of that same house. Carla was nine months pregnant with her first child at the time and couldn't travel to attend her brother's funeral. Both of her losses were involuntary, unanticipated, and arguably more traumatic than my own had been. The joy of giving birth, her emotional well-being, her profound faith, and a strong support system allowed Carla to handle the multiple losses in a graceful manner that quite frankly awed me. She savored the blessing of bringing her son into the world rather than dwelling on not being able to share the moment with her mother and brother.

> **"The best way to cheer yourself up is
> to cheer somebody else up."**
> —Mark Twain

My experience has taught me that bad things do happen to good people and that we all need to see the good in the bad—the opportunity to grow, to help others, or to grow by helping others.

Da Nile

> "The only atheism is the denial of truth."
> —Arthur Lynch

A commonly experienced blender setting worthy of special mention is denial. I definitely have written the book on this one. When my career crisis came, I was very careful to tell people that I *chose* to leave the bank, that the executive managers all but begged me not to, and that I could have stayed on in a different capacity if I had felt like it. There was some truth to this "glass is half full" view. I was offered three alternative positions, all of which were lateral moves involving relocation. Then, the human resources folks kind of lost their sense of humor; it was a bit like baseball ("three strikes, and you're out"). Luckily for me, I was out with some benefits (not a golden parachute but more like a colorful umbrella that garnishes a cocktail), thanks to the nineteen years I had put in. The silver lining of this phase was the summer I was able to spend with my sons, who were then six and eight. I received my sixty-day's notice in early May, a month before they got out of school for the summer. It was the first summer that I had spent with them, and I treasured every minute. The other mothers basically thought I was insane, but I think it was just my manic phase.

In spite of my high spirits, however, I was decidedly in denial. Provided with the full array of outplacement services at a reputable local firm, I never used the available office space and rarely interacted with the consultant assigned to me because that was what fired people did. *I* wasn't fired; I was severed, which now that I think about it sounds even more gruesome. I did the usual things, like take a battery of assessments, but stubbornly decided to sort things out on my own.

> "I believe in looking reality straight
> in the eye and denying it."
> —Garrison Keillor

Denial is a universally experienced emotional state particularly when a shock loss occurs.

When I met my client Margaret, her husband had died unexpectedly ten years earlier at age thirty-eight. For the first two years after his death, she visited his grave and talked to him for the better part of the day. She took him blankets when it was cold and even brought him food and clothing on occasion. Others around her slowly convinced her that she needed to spend more time on building a new life for herself, and over the next three months, she weaned herself off of the daily cemetery visits and began to enjoy the company of friends. This helped her accept that her husband was gone rather than deny that reality.

My father handled my mother's death quite differently. When the doctors diagnosed my mother with lung cancer, the oncologists gave her a prognosis of eight to twelve months because she had multiple tumors in her brain at the time the cancer was found. My father tried to maintain their customary lifestyle during the almost nine months that she lived, including taking her out to their favorite haunts until it became impossible. The day after she died, he all but chased us off, not so that he could grieve privately, but so he could conduct his daily routine in a business-as-usual manner. Even though he had nine months of warning, I believe that he had been in denial of her death. He never admitted it because he also was in denial of the denial, which is always the case; that is what makes it the long and winding "Da Nile."

For a less morbid example, Don, a former colleague was told that his position was going to be eliminated after fifteen years of service at the bank. He reacted by returning to his office as though nothing had happened. He didn't tell his wife what had transpired but continued to go to the office every day during his notice period and interact with peers as if nothing had changed. The day he packed his personal effects, he said his good-byes as though they were simply good nights and headed home. He actually remained in denial until anxiety began to seep in, and he moved into the next blender phase.

Clearly, the progression through the transition model is not always linear but more cyclical or curvilinear. Even after you reach digestion, you can always slip back into the blender, be it denial or any other setting.

Forget Da Nile—How About Rio Real?

> "Reality is merely an illusion, albeit
> a very persistent one."
> —Albert Einstein

When denial starts to fade, this little thing called reality usually starts to sink it. This is the whip setting on your blender, representing an emotional downturn as you get whipped back to reality. Common emotions during this period are anxiety, confusion, depression, and the loss of self-confidence. For example, the death of a partner (like Margaret's story above) might invoke sadness and fear of being on your own. After the initial flurry of activity to get the deceased's affairs in order, it grows awfully quiet. Once the sympathy-bearers go back home, the days become a bit lonely. Another example is that after you give birth, and you suddenly realize that you actually have to take care of this child for at least the next eighteen years. This revelation makes you question your ability to do so, particularly if the baby is colicky. Or following a job loss, you might become concerned about your ability to stay afloat financially.

In my case, I was extremely fortunate to have adequate financial support to alleviate my concerns about providing for two children at least in the near term. When the end of that first free summer came into sight, I started to feel anxious about what I was going to do when the kids went back to school. Echoing values instilled during my childhood, my inner voice cries out, "Achieve! Achieve! Achieve!"—and did I mention, "Achieve!"? And so the garden club, the tennis team, or a daytime talk show (except as a host or guest) wasn't in the cards (gosh, I never thought about the bridge club) for me.

Have you ever known anyone (not from a supermarket tabloid but a real person) who has gotten married suddenly and then plunged into ambivalence after the honeymoon? I actually do. Linda had known her future husband for months when they somewhat impulsively decided to get married in a small family-only ceremony. After the reception, they took a trip to California to celebrate their new state of marital bliss. During the honeymoon, the couple irritated each other so intensely that they literally flew home in separate sections of the jumbo jet and didn't converse at all during the long flight. The good news is that they are still married eighteen years later because they subsequently worked through the transition to married life.

I witnessed a lot of uncertainty, anxiety, and/or self-doubt during the two-year period I stayed on after the bank for which I had worked was acquired by one institution and then merged with Bank of America. Within a couple of years, the company went from a $42 billion financial institution with core banking operations in Florida only to the second largest bank in the United States with a global presence in many lines of business. I saw a number of colleagues leave the company, sometimes by choice but more often not of their own volition. Like me, several went through the honeymoon phase following their departure but ended up agitated, anxious, or apprehensive at some point, often when severance pay ran out.

For example, Doug left the organization after they eliminated his job and offered him an early retirement package, which provided salary and benefits for the subsequent six months. During that time, he got to work out, play golf, and see his children more than he had before. His full-time working spouse began to get resentful of his freedom and anxious that she might become the sole breadwinner. As the end of his severance period approached, her anxiety perhaps became infectious, and he became uncertain and worried about his and his family's future.

"The highest reward for man's toil is not what
he gets for it but what he becomes by it."
—John Ruskin

The return of the difficult blender period is that the related emotions, like the pancake ingredients, need to be processed and left behind. You can be whipped, beaten, shaken, or stirred but emerge almost smooth with perhaps just a few small bumps. Again, common feelings experienced during these times are anger, sadness, grief, loneliness, and fear, or relief, excitement, hope, optimism, and confidence. As time goes by, you are able to detach these emotions from the event. For example, if you are unexpectedly fired from your job, you might be shocked, angry, resentful, and afraid. You might have difficulty eating, sleeping, or enjoying activities that usually give you pleasure. At some point, however, the strong emotions will subside, and you will remember the event (being fired) without feeling the emotions. This is partly because you have worked through them during the blender stage.

Have you ever had a relationship end and felt as though your life had come to a halt and that your broken heart would never mend? I hear clients say all of the time that their lives will *never* be the same, that they won't *ever* recover, and that they will feel this way *forever*. For most, or at least for those without enduring mental health or other challenges, time does heal almost all wounds, albeit slowly in some cases. Here are some examples.

Ellen had an extraarital affair, which went on for almost a year. Her lover abruptly broke off the relationship by leaving her a cryptic voicemail message and never spoke to her again. She wasn't able to get the closure that she wanted in order to move on and swore that she would "never" be the same. As time marched on, however, her feelings of confusion and hurt lessened in intensity, and she was able to remember the relationship without feeling the strong emotions. It was especially challenging for her because the affair had been a secret, and, therefore, she had no confidants (or confidence, for that matter) to help her through her dejection. In counseling, she was able to work through the feelings of hurt, abandonment, and depression that she felt and move on with her life rather than remain stagnant.

Ron was stunned one evening when his wife of fifteen years asked him for a divorce. He was certain that she must have found someone else and even hired a private investigator to check out his hunch. His hurt turned to anger, and he retained a high-priced lawyer to sue for custody of their two children. After a bitter and expensive battle, he started to accept the situation. In time, he was able to rebound from his anger and hurt and even resume romantic involvement with other women. After a year or so, he realized that the breakup actually was a positive step for all involved and was able to let go of the emotions of the event.

> "When one door of happiness closes, another opens;
> but often we look so long at the closed door that
> we do not see the one which has opened for us."
> —Helen Keller

So, how do you survive the stressful mixture of emotions which characterize the blender? First, take a reasonable amount of time to process your feelings. Second, try to start moving forward when you feel like you're stuck, sulking in your tent, or wallowing in self-pity. Third, seek the support of family and/or friends to help you get through this period. It might be beneficial to get counseling, be it through a coach, pastor, priest, psychotherapist, or rabbi. This may help to restore your faith in a higher power, yourself, and your future and provide objective assistance of those who are not as close to you. For those who have trouble functioning or experiencing pleasure, professional help is highly beneficial. Alternatively, you can find healing in prayer, meditation, or other forms of relaxation on your own (see the Every Breath You Take section of this chapter for specific techniques). It also is helpful for some to keep a journal during this period. Journaling can heighten your awareness of your thoughts and feelings, which is a great first step down the road to recovery.

"Journal writing is a voyage to the interior."

—Christina Baldwin

Simply stated, two of the best tools to help you through the blender stage are both free and readily available. These utensils are your mind and your body, your thoughts and your actions. We are going to cover mind and body exercises in the sections which follow.

Food for Thought

"The greatest discovery of my generation
is that a human being can alter his life
by altering his attitudes of mind."
—William James

An effective, user-friendly antidote for self-defeating or other negative blender emotions is *self-talk*, otherwise known as cognitive behavioral therapy (CBT), a widely practiced, empirically validated, and long-lasting form of psychotherapy. Cognitive behavioral therapy seeks to identify and change distorted, unhealthy, unrealistic ways of thinking in order to influence emotion and behavior. Cognitive or thought restructuring is essential to a successful life transition during which your concepts of self and the environment shift. In fact, transition can't take place without reframing your thoughts and changing your behavior. For example, if you look at that first pancake, you could say to yourself, "I will never make a decent pancake. I am a lousy cook, and I am not going to cook anymore," or you could say, "Glad I got the test cake out of the way because now, the griddle is ready to make beauties, and I think I'll take a cooking class to perfect my skills." These alternative ways of interpreting the same event (the first pancake) make you feel and—by extension—act very differently. In the first scenario, your negative thoughts cause you to feel unmotivated and, in turn, to stop cooking. In the second, your more optimistic thoughts make you feel inspired, and you start to cook and to want to improve, grow, and develop. I vote for the thoughts and action behind door number two, and I am certain that you do too.

For another example beyond the kitchen, let's imagine that you are let go by your employer. If you think that you lost your job because you were inferior to your colleagues, you probably feel inadequate in some manner and aren't motivated to try to find a new job. After all, who would want to hire you? You don't respond to ads or make any calls during the ensuing weeks because you do not want to set yourself up to fail or to be rejected again. The negative thought about why your company let you go causes you to feel depressed; in turn, your sadness causes you to retreat. Or worse, you conclude that because you were fired, you will *never* get another job and, therefore, your productive life has come to a halt. In this scenario, you're overgeneralizing by interpreting a single event as an irreversible, ongoing pattern.

By viewing the same event in a more positive light (for example, I lost my job because the company downsized), you will probably feel better and act accordingly. Think of the time between jobs as a well-earned sabbatical rather than the end of the world, and you can lift your mood with positive thoughts and constructive action.

The first step of CBT is to capture your thoughts. This sounds simple but actually can be very hard to do because we each have tens of thousands of thoughts per day. Our thoughts are automatic; they just pop into our heads. In order to catch these thoughts, you need to slow down, pay attention, and listen to the silence. Once you identify a thought, consider how it is making you feel. Or when you identify a feeling in your heart, try to identify the accompanying thought in your head.

Oftentimes if the emotion is negative, it is because the thought in your head is illogical or distorted. Cognitive therapists, beginning with Aaron Beck and continuing more recently with David Burns, MD,point out common thinking errors including the following:

- **Black or White Thinking:** This is thinking in extremes. The first pancake stinks or is great. There is no in-between. You're either good or bad; people love you or they hate you; you're a success or a failure. You are a hard-core extremist.
- **Negative Nelly**: This is the Chicken Little (a.k.a. the sky is falling) error. You take one negative event and turn it into a personal never-ending pattern. The pancake is ugly, and you will *never* cook anything decent. For example, you get fired, and you will *never* get another job. Your child gets in trouble at school, and he *always* will be a troublemaker.

- **Selective Hearing:** This means disregarding the positive and focusing on the negative. The last pancake you made looks terrific, but you still focus on the first crummy one you made. For example, during your performance review, your boss praises you in several areas but suggests that you could have done better with your presentations. You subsequently ruminate about the presentations and all but forget the praise.
- **Lipstick on the Collar:** These are the times when you interpret things negatively even though there is no supporting evidence. You throw out the first pancake because you are so sure that no one, not even your dog, is going to eat it. I don't know about you but my dog loves pancakes, even the first one, especially with a dollop of syrup; yet you just toss it in the trashcan. For example, you're invited to a party, but you don't want to go because you know that you won't have a good time.
- **Should-ing on Yourself:** These are the should, must, or ought statements that make you feel guilty or just plain bad. The first pancake didn't turn out well, so I *should* have waited for the griddle to heat longer (or bought the ready-mades you just pop in the microwave). Women are particularly skilled at this one. I am fourteen, so I should have my period. I am twenty-eight so I should be married. I am thirty so I should have children by now. I am fifty-one so I should have gone through menopause. According to whom? And are these events really within your control? Stop should-ding all over yourself please, you deserve better.
- **Sticks and Stones:** This is what we tell children not to do—name-calling. I can't make pancakes, so I am a bad wife and mother. This is when you lose one tennis match and call yourself a loser. Or you make one mistake and refer to yourself as a failure. It's an extreme form of the black-or-white thinking noted above. Placing names or labels on others creates negative emotions as well.
- **All About Me:** This is the "it's all my fault" feeling you get sometimes even though you aren't necessarily to blame. This faux pas is putting yourself at the center of the universe by taking things personally or taking blame for things that aren't

your fault. It's my fault that the first pancake looks silly when, in fact, the first one always does—it's a law of science. For example, I'm so sorry that it's raining at my outdoor party. I should have known better and had it indoors.

I am confident that some or all of these distortions hit home with you. Although it's good to be aware of them, please don't get caught up in the terms or memorizing all of the semantics. The important thing is that you recognize that some of your thoughts that cause you to feel bad are illogical. The next step is to reframe those quirky thoughts so that you will feel better and to behave in ways that don't promote dysfunctional thinking.

I advocate five ideas, in keeping with the five-stage pancake model, to reframe your thoughts. When you feel bad, ask yourself:

1. What am I thinking?
2. How is that thought making me feel?
3. What is the evidence for and against the accompanying thought?
4. Would I voice this thought to a friend?
5. Is there an alternative thought that would make me feel better?

For example, if you send someone an e-mail or leave a voicemail but receive no response, you might conclude that he doesn't care enough to respond, that he thought your message was stupid, or that you must have done something to offend him. These thoughts probably make you feel sad, depressed, or rejected. Ponder the evidence for and against your thought. There is probably no truly conclusive evidence because at this point, it's just jumping to conclusions, as with lipstick on the collar. If a friend told you this had happened to her, would you say, "You're right. He hates your guts"? I strongly doubt it. You might suggest that he is busy, that he has just experienced some personal crisis, or perhaps his car, cell phone, or computer has crashed. If you wouldn't say this to a friend, why in the world would you say it to yourself? And so what if he doesn't respond? Does this mean that you're a failure and unworthy of anyone's attention? An alternative hypothesis (like that *he* isn't worthy of your attention) can greatly change your thought and improve your mood.

Recipe: Thought Reframing Steps

1. What am I thinking?

2. How is that thought making me feel?

3. What is the evidence for and against the accompanying thought?

4. Would I voice this thought to a friend?

5. Is there an alternative thought that would make me feel better?

"Our life is what our thoughts make it."
—Marcus Aurelius

In sum, even this nutshell version of CBT can really help work through the negative moods experienced during the blender stage and, for that matter, the rest of your stack of pancakes. Try to become aware of your thoughts, consider how they are making you feel, and change the way you feel for the better. Heightening your self-awareness is a learned skill that we will discuss later. For now, focus on what you are thinking, how it makes you feel, what actual evidence supports the thought, would you say what you are thinking to a friend, and what is an alternative thought that would make you feel better.

CBT is a learned skill, and you really hone your skills if you do your homework and practice. One of my favorite CBT self-help books is *The Feeling Good Handbook* by Dr. David D. Burns. Like many books of this genre, *The Feeling Good Handbook* contains some action-provoking exercises to make the ideas real. Although it is useful to read self-help books, it is far better to read them and actually *do* the prescribed exercises, which is why many self-help books are called *workbooks*. I mean do you look like the person on the cover after simply reading a fitness magazine? No, so we actually have to do those wretched exercises. Once you master the art of CBT, the awareness of your thoughts and amending the distortions thereof will become automatic. Then, you'll have more time for physical fitness exercises, which some of you may view as a punishment, but which will, I promise you, lift your mood too. (CBT topics worthy of your time can be found in the Recommended Resources in the appendices.)

To try your hand at CBT, try to complete several exercises like the following example:

Event

Throw out the first pancake.

Thought

I am a lousy cook, and I don't know what to serve for breakfast now.

Feeling

Anxious about waiting, afraid of disappointing hungry family members, depressed that I am not a better cook, and resentful that I am the only one who ever makes breakfast.

Action

Throw away the remaining batter and take out breakfast cereal.

Alternative Thought

Great! Now the griddle is the right heat and ready to make beautiful, golden pancakes.

Alternative Feeling

Hopeful, excited, optimistic, and motivated to keep cooking, and go for the perfect pancake(s).

Alternative Action

Stir the batter, create golden pancakes, and enjoy!

"Life is too important to take seriously."
—Corky Siegel

I believe that humor also is a powerful mind-bending tool for coping with the emotions of the blender stage. It's okay to lose your mind, but do whatever you can to preserve your sense of humor, particularly about yourself. Watch a funny movie, read a humorous book, glance at some cartoons, or just surround yourself with people who energize you and make you laugh. Laugh out loud and smile wide—you may even count that as prescribed exercise if you don't happen to be a cardio aficionado, gym rat, or jock. There are research studies which prove that laughter is medicine. Laughter actually can lower blood pressure, stress-hormone levels, and even prevent heart attacks by exercising the lungs, belly, heart, and soul.

Big Screen Theory

Speaking of funny movies, I am disadvantaged by not knowing you well enough to select specific mood movies for you. I am confident that you've heard of cinematherapy, and I hope that you also have tried it out. Cinematherapy actually refers to what its name implies, the therapeutic or healing use of film. I'm willing to bet that you can think of a time when you cried your eyes out after a moving movie or busted a gut laughing over a funny film. If not, it has been too long since you have seen a touching movie, be it on the big screen down the block or in the comfort of your home. Cinematherapy is sometimes used as an adjunct to counseling provided by a third party, usually as homework assigned in between sessions and then debriefed upon completion. Alternatively, cinematherapy can be self-administered in accordance with the recommendations below. The benefits include insight, or at least comfort, provided by identifying with a character or situation; the release of tension either through laughter or tears; and developing the skill of seeing yourself and others more objectively.

According to www.cinematherapy.com, watching a movie can engage all seven of our intelligences: the logical (plot), the linguistic (dialogues), the visual-spatial (pictures, colors, and symbols), the musical (sounds and music), the interpersonal (storytelling), the body-kinesthetic (moving), and the intrapersonal (inner guidance). The theory of these multiple intelligences was originally presented by Harvard-based psychologist Howard Gardner in his book *Frames of Mind: The Theory of Multiple Intelligences.* Cinematherapy, thus, benefits our emotional well-being, cognitive skills, and multiple intelligences.. All of that plus great snacks, which you need to enjoy mindfully as we will discuss.

Prescription Popcorn

- Sit as comfortably as you can and take a few deep abdominal breaths. Try to release any tension you feel in your body. Relax.
- Have pleasing refreshments on hand to enjoy mindfully. Remember to savor each and every kernel or Raisinet. They only live once.
- Focus your attention on the movie that you're watching, but don't analyze or judge as you view.
- Pay attention to your feelings during and after the film. Notice the pace of your breathing or other outwardly expressed emotions (like laughing or crying).
- Talk about your feelings afterward with a companion, third party, or journal. Reflect on your thoughts and opinions about the film, and consider any insights you might have.
- Consider what you gained from the movie. Even if you hated it, that feeling probably tells you something about yourself.

"Happiness comes from spiritual wealth. Happiness
comes from giving, not getting. If we try hard
to bring happiness to others, we cannot stop
it from coming to us also. To get joy, we must
give it, and to keep joy, we must scatter it."
—John Templeton

Another cinematherapy exercise is to take children between seven and eleven to the movies. I mean between ages seven and eleven, not between seven and eleven pm, especially on school nights. Why? Because, according to Jean Piaget, children around this age are still in the concrete operations stage of critical thinking, which means their capacity to reason is growing like a weed, yet they aren't capable of abstract thought. Therefore, they're in awe of the big screen. If observing their incredible blossoming brains and fantastic faces at work isn't enough for you, you may just luck out when they get scared or otherwise moved and give you a tender caress. Of course, I can't speak to kisses, because I have sons, and the movie theater is public domain. Accordingly, I've borrowed girls from dear friends to experiment and test the validity of my big screen hypothesis using different cohorts. Please try this one at home. If you don't have children, borrow some. I can assure that you that their parents are happy to loan them to you, which doubles your jackpot because you also enjoy the rewards of doing something for a friend. Taking children older than age eleven also is fun because they can be abstract thinkers, but they're so old that their parents no longer need babysitters.

> **"Outside of a dog, a book is man's best friend.**
> **Inside of a dog, it's too dark to read."**
> —Groucho Mark

An alternative to getting lost in a movie is becoming engrossed in a book (as I'm confident you are at this moment). What a novel idea! Actually, reading any type of book can help alter your mood by allowing you to identify with a character or the material, release pent-up emotions (also known as catharsis), and, accordingly, gain insights into your own issues. In simplest terms, bibliotherapy refers to the selection of reading material that is relevant to an individual's life situation and will therefore be therapeutic to him or her. Bibliotherapy can consist of reading, discussion, and/or writing. Sometimes a therapist can assign reading for someone, which they can go over during future sessions. In addition, individuals can just read on their own without a therapist's intervention, especially given the vast number of available self-help books. Other opportunities are in book clubs in your community or online. These are ways to process your thoughts and emotions after you've read a book. You can always start a book club if you can't find one you like. In short, reading is beneficial as an adjunct to therapy or a stand-alone exercise. In either case, reading can help you cope with various life events, including life transitions. Bibliotherapy, with or without therapeutic intervention, is a healing experience during the blender stage or another stage. I've found reading helpful for a number of my clients who are motivated to work at change.

The fact is that reading books about transition during a transition period will be good for your mental health if for no other reason because misery loves company, and you can identify with the topic or the characters. In addition, consider this: if the author actually is in sound enough condition to write a book, chances are that you can make it through your transition, too. The recommended resources list in the appendices provides you with what is hopefully an inspirational list of recommended material.

Body Works

"Reading is to the mind what exercise is to the body"
—Sir Richard Steele

Having covered how you can use your mind (especially if you lose it in the blender) to positively influence your mood, we will now discuss how you can use your body to your benefit. I'm going to advocate two seemingly contradictory ideas—exercise and relaxation. These activities actually complement each other and are equally beneficial for combating stress, anxiety, depression, and a host of physiological and psychological conditions. Remember that transition is widely recognized as a source of major stress.

As hard as it may be, try to stay energized by taking care of yourself with proper food, rest, and exercise. This doesn't mean that you have to join an expensive gym or sweat until you drop. Even a fifteen-minute walk can revitalize you because physical activity releases chemicals in the brain that inhibit pain signals and produce pleasure. There is a wealth of empirical research validating that exercise can be as effective as antidepressants in elevating mood. So I urge you to kindly get moving.

You also don't have to join a club to relax because you already possess a good and readily available tool to practice relaxation—your body. Of course, this costs you nothing because you already own it, and hopefully, in accordance with advice provided above, you're taking great care of your body. When you're stressed, please pay attention to the signals your body sends, indicating that you need to relax like tension in the neck or face, a pounding heart, a mild headache, or an upset stomach. Once you recognize the physical manifestations of these uncomfortable emotions, you can learn to practice relaxation in order to prevent stress from affecting you in this manner.

Personally, I used to be very cynical about relaxation techniques. I actually left my first Lamaze class at the break because I thought, "Forget about telling me to breathe. I've been doing that for thirty-something years; just give me the epidural and put me out of my misery." Older and wiser now, I don't recommend this to others because I practically had sweet Reid in the car on the way to the hospital and while en route I was more screaming than breathing mindfully. Perhaps I should've finished that class instead of some of the less practical ones in high school, college, and beyond.

On another occasion, I was on a business trip and ducked into the airport gift shop to get souvenirs for the boys. At the checkout counter, I bought a book for myself called *How to Overcome Your Fear of Flying*. I was *so* afraid of flying for all of the reasons they cited in the book (like you are a control freak, claustrophobic, or afraid of dying). When I got to the relaxation suggestions, I completely checked out because it wasn't *my* cup of tea. Well, guess what? I finally drank the Kool-Aid, and now, I'm hooked. I'm a relaxation practitioner and proponent.

> **"During [these] periods of relaxation after concentrated intellectual activity, the intuitive mind seems to take over and can produce the sudden clarifying insights, which give so much joy and delight."**
> —Fritjof Capra

It is much easier to cover what relaxation can't help with than what benefits it offers. During life transitions, relaxation can relieve the stressful emotions you experience during the blender stage and allow you to get in touch with your thoughts and feelings. This, in turn, lets you make more perfect pancakes. In general, relaxation offers psychological and physiological benefits, and practitioners use it clinically to treat an expanding range of problems, including chronic pain, diabetes, asthma, cardiovascular disease, immune system deficiencies, stress, anxiety, depression, and panic attacks.

How does it work? The sympathetic nervous system reacts to stress by secreting hormones (cortisol and noripenephrine) that prepare the body to face a perceived threat. This is the "fight-or-flight" response identified in the early 1900's by Harvard physiologist Walter B. Cannon. The accompanying physiological changes can include an increased heart rate, sweating, fast breathing, blood rushing to the extremities, and the tensing of muscles. The way to shut this stress response down is to invoke what Herbert Benson termed the *relaxation response* in his book of the same name. You can effectively use your mind to change your physiology because once you think that a situation isn't dangerous, your brain stops the panic signals to the nervous system and you slow down. By invoking the relaxation response, you can restore your body to its non-fight-or-flight, healthier state.

A simple way to understand the difference between tension and relaxation is (after you finish reading this short paragraph) to shut your eyes really tight and experience how that feels. Feel the tension in your face and your forehead, and notice how uncomfortable it feels. Now, open your eyes and relax the eyelids. Notice how much more soothing you feel as you loosen those muscles and become more relaxed.

The benefits of relaxation have been so widely recognized and accepted that practitioners have developed a number of different relaxation techniques now in vogue. Some of these practices include deep breathing, progressive muscle relaxation, biofeedback, humor, meditation, massage, yoga, self-hypnosis, visualization, prayer, and music. I'm going to provide you with a couple of basic relaxation exercises to get you started.

Like any skill, relaxation must be learned; it isn't an innate ability. Do you really think that being born was relaxing? You most likely were as stressed as your mother was, but you were just unable to articulate your feelings at the time. Essentially, you can begin to learn how to relax through deep abdominal breathing. This is a good choice because it is short, simple, and adaptable to almost any setting.

Every Breath You Take

- Lie down (if at all possible) or sit in a comfortable position without crossing your arms and legs.
- Keep your spine straight.
- Place one hand on your chest and the other on your abdomen.
- Notice any muscle tension that you are feeling.
- Inhale slowly and deeply through your nose. The hand on your abdomen should rise, but the hand on your chest should move ever so slightly, if at all.
- Inhale until your abdomen pushes against your hand as much as you feel comfortable.
- Hold the breath in your belly. Try to count to five (one, one hundred; two, one hundred; and so on) before beginning to exhale.
- Exhale through your mouth as though you're trying to cool down a spoonful of hot liquid. Enjoy the wonderful whooshing sound of exhalation.
- Notice the tension leaving your jaw and face muscles as you exhale.
- Repeat at least five times.

Five-Five-Ten

I would like to propose the following easy way to remember a breathing exercise.

- Breathe in through the nose for a count of five.
- Hold the breath for a count of five.
- Exhale for a count of ten.

If you have more time—about twenty minutes—the following exercise would be beneficial:

Recipe: Deep Breathing for Five-Five-Ten

- Breathe in through the nose for a count of five.

- Hold the breath for a count of five.

- Exhale for a count of ten.

Progressive Muscle Relaxation

Edmund Jacobson developed this technique to teach individuals how to relax their muscles and ease the accompanying tension by performing relaxation techniques for different parts of the body, which allows you to release the tension slowly throughout the whole body. This exercise teaches you the difference between the stressful sensation of tension and the more soothing feeling of relaxation. Don't attempt any of these exercises if you think that they might cause you any discomfort, and feel free to modify them to fit your own body and relaxation program. This might be best done with a partner who can guide you through the steps, or you can purchase a relaxation tape to be your guide.

- Sit in a comfortable chair with your head supported, or lie down and be as comfortable as possible. Take a few deep abdominal breaths, and begin to relax.
- Make a fist with one hand, and feel the tension in the wrist and forearm. Extend the fingers, release, and relax. Repeat with other hand.
- Make a fist again and tense your bicep by raising your fist toward your shoulder. Then, drop your arm to your side, release your fingers, and relax. Repeat with other arm.
- Shrug your shoulders up toward your ears and hold them there tightly. Now, drop the shoulders, and relax.
- Turn your head to the right and hold the tension, then turn to the left, and finally lower your chin to your chest. Notice the unpleasant sensation in your neck, then return your head to an upright position, and relax.
- Close your eyes as tightly as you can, and hold. Now, open your eyes, and relax.
- Clench your jaw as tightly as you can, and experience the stress. Now, let go, let your jaw drop and your mouth open, and relax.
- Purse your lips together as snug as you can, then let go, and relax your mouth.
- Tense your buttock muscles as hard as you can, press your buttocks into the chair, then release, and relax.

- Dig your heels into the floor, feeling the tightness in your thighs; hold, then release, and relax.
- Pull your stomach in as far as you can—imagine that you're trying to push your navel into your spine. Then, let go, loosen the stomach muscles, and relax.
- Flex your foot toward your body, hold the tension in your calves, then drop your foot, and relax.
- Take a few more deep abdominal breaths, and enjoy the deep relaxation of your body.

Once you've mastered these exercises, you can use any or all of them to shut down the developing physiological signals of tension. Better yet, perform relaxation proactively and preventively to keep well and ward off stress. If you are pressed for time, just tense and relax a few muscles. Check it out because it really works.

Image-Creation

> "I am enough of an artist to draw freely upon my imagination. Imagination is more important than knowledge. Knowledge is limited. Imagination encircles the world."
> —Albert Einstein

Visualization or imagery is a valuable add-on to breathing or other forms of relaxation. By creating a picture in your mind, you can invoke the relaxation response, shutting down stress and its physiological changes. For example, when I fly and we encounter turbulence, I close my eyes, focus on my breathing, and picture myself at the baggage claim where I'm safe, on the ground, and, most importantly, alive. Once I do that, I'm able to enjoy the rest of the trip (until the flight home, of course). Or when I am in bad traffic, I tend to panic that I'm going to be late to an appointment, so I draw a few abdominal breaths, picture a safe arrival at my destination, and say to myself, "So what if I am late?

Will my life be over? Will the world stop turning? I hardly think so." This reframes my mental state and puts me at ease.

One basic visualization exercise is to create your own mental sanctuary. This is a place where you feel safe, comfortable, content, and are able to relax. For me, sunsets, especially the ones I remember from my childhood, are my temple. I had the pleasure and privilege of mindfully watching the sun set over Clear Lake many times and enjoying each dusk-to-darkness experience for its unique beauty. Now, when I want to really relax, I gently close my eyes and imagine that I'm seated on the dock, feeling the moist wood underneath me. I gaze out to the west and watch the sky turn spectacular shades of red, orange, pink, and purple. White streaks of cloud become gray, pink, black, and then almost invisible as darkness approaches. The orange sun expands and then contracts as it starts to sink slowly into the water. Loons cry out into the night as if to warn the lake of the sun's approach. The smell of birch, pine, and soil engulf me. Right before the sun hits the lake, I slide off the dock into the water to enjoy a bedtime dip. Completely at peace and pleasantly tired from a happy day with friends, I'm ready to sink into the comfort of my bed. Soft sheets and the cozy quilt surround me before I doze off—deeper, deeper, and deeper into sleep. (As an aside, the lake is in Canada, and so in spite of the heat of the sun, the water temperature wasn't for the faint of heart.)

That is my sanctuary: your safe place is your own; you need to create it and practice deeply thinking about its sights, sounds, smells, and/or tastes. If your image is an airplane, a labor and delivery room, or a blender, more power to you. This is a custom-built tool, and I commend you for creating it; the payoff is well worth your effort. Let me just recommend a warm bath instead of a freezing swim at the end of your mental movie.

Instead of an entire mental movie, you can just use individual scenes to alter your mood. Recently, I ran in a couple of half-marathons, and my younger son told me that he would give me a hug if I bettered my time in the second race. Every time I felt myself dragging, I pictured myself walking into the house, declaring that I had achieved the goal he set for me, and collecting my hug. That image helped me to pick up the pace.

This type of visualization can be very helpful in shaping the next chapter of your life after you emerge from the blender stage. Is this what your perfect pancake looks like? Who is in your life in this scenario? Where are you living? What are you doing?

Sometimes It's Hard to Be a Woman

Before we leave the blender stage, and at the risk of alienating any male readers, I'm going to devote the next section to the unique life transitions that occur when a woman becomes a mother, acquires an empty nest, or undergoes a drastic hormonal change. Women actually seem to corner the market on major life transitions and accordingly spend a disproportionate amount of time in the blender stage. Just look at the pancake section of your local market. There, you'll find Aunt Jemima's fixings, Mrs. Butterworth's syrup, Sue Bee Honey, and Grandma's Molasses. There's not a guy in sight. Guys, before you start that fast-forward channel-flip thing, kindly pause for thought. Please don't hit the mute button. Even if you aren't a woman, you most likely know at least one. If you can better understand her, you can provide her with more support. She, in turn, will be appreciative and want to meet *your* needs, which will result in everyone's living happily ever after. So, please stay tuned through these next few sections.

Parent Pancake

Adopting, birthing, or otherwise acquiring children dramatically changes your lifestyle. In terms of the blender stage, becoming a parent may take the pancake. Certainly, giving birth is a unique life experience. When I was pregnant, I read that wonderful *What to Expect When You're Expecting* book, except for the chapters on labor and delivery because those made me panic. As I mentioned before, I should've stayed in that Lamaze class and learned how *not* to panic. Instead, I asked a colleague with children what the delivery felt like, and she said, "Just imagine pooping out a watermelon." Ouch. Fortunately, my first son, Gray, was more like a cantaloupe, and Reid was a honeydew, so actually I was pleasantly surprised.

I also have several friends who have adopted children. I always love to learn of an adoption, in part because my mother was adopted but also because it's a win-win for the parents and the child. Even though adopting parents don't technically give birth, their lifestyle undergoes the same seismic shift. It can be even more abrupt if, after a long waiting period, suddenly you get that call.

Just ask Rob and Terry who decided to adopt and a only few weeks later and under highly unusual circumstances adopted two brothers. *A few weeks*—often people wait years. Both parents were in their forties at the time and had never had children. Talk about a lifestyle change, and trust me we're less flexible in midlife than in earlier eras. Terry lost quite a bit of weight in the ensuing months because she found herself too busy to eat. She also almost lost her mind on several occasions as she adjusted to the demands the boys made of her, but she never lost sight of the blessing it was to have them after a decade of unsuccessfully trying to get pregnant.

I understand that life changes for both partners, no matter their gender; in fact, the whole household dynamic shifts. I truly believe, though, that even now, the woman still undergoes greater emotional upheaval than the man does. It's like men go through the blender stage on the mix or blend setting while women are on the crush and grate speeds. If you give birth, of course, you can write it off as raging hormones or sleep deprivation, which can make just about anyone a raging maniac.

> **"Life is something that happens to you when you can't get to sleep."**
> —Fran Lebowitz

Whether you're working in or out of your house you certainly will face major life transitions when children come along. As we discussed earlier, I happened to be working when I gave birth to both of my sons. This was not due to chance, rather I had been overachieving at the office for sixteen years before my first son. A working woman is faced with a multitude of options like remaining employed outside of the home, cutting back to part-time, quitting, making a career transition, taking a short or long leave or immediately returning to work and telling the father to deal with it on her way out the door. And this is just the beginning; for example, if you work at all from home, who will care for the child while you are busy? Should you return to work outside of the home? How do you manage that transition? If and when do you put the child in daycare or preschool, which one and how do you get her there and pick her up? What do you pack for snack, yours and hers?

> **"Funny business, a woman's career; the things you drop on the way up the ladder, so you can move faster. You forget you'll need them again when you get back to being a woman. It's one career all females have in common, whether we like it or not; being a woman. Sooner or later, we've got to work at it, no matter how many other careers we've had or wanted."**
> —Joseph L. Mankiewicz

My solution—to remain employed full-time and have a second child twenty-three months later—was a somewhat mindless one. This leads to another issue that women face: managing their hormonal swings and emotions from the blender stage in front of male co-workers and even bosses. When I informed my boss that I was expecting a second child, he digested that news flash for thirty days before giving me a lateral demotion, which is my term for a different position with the same pay grade and title to cover up the status downgrade. He was a smart guy because had he cut my pay that surely would have been discrimination and I could have retired on the financial rewards from my lawsuit. He sketched out the old job-new job scenario on his own personal grease-board (apparently he thought I was either a visual learner or a complete moron). Having worked my way up the ladder for twelve years, I was so infuriated by his insulting insinuation that I couldn't perform my job while raising two infants that I unloaded on him in pretty colorful language. Obviously, I had yet to perfect my relaxation skills and allowed my emotions to take over. Maybe part of my anger came because I thought that maybe he could be right. I felt so conflicted about whether I wanted to be the Chairman of the bank or the playground. My sleep patterns also changed because I got none for approximately the next three to five years. I took on a new identity as a mom, which conflicted a bit with my CEO aspirations. The fight between my need to achieve and my desire to be with my children went on for several rounds. Actually, it was draining in every sense of the word—a veritable high-speed blender cycle with a divine intervention (my severance) pulling the plug out for me.

After Reid was born, I decided to take a whopping four full weeks off before easing back into my new lower-responsibility job, initially part-time. During the four-week hiatus, I borrowed a laptop computer, which I basically had no idea how to use. I still have a touch of post-traumatic stress when I relive moments of this self-inflicted experience like the image of nursing Reid while using my big toe to answer e-mail and consoling Gray who wanted more attention. I was so physically, mentally, and emotionally exhausted that I couldn't see the light at the top of the blender. My inner voice didn't allow me to do what I had encouraged other female colleagues and friends to do—to relax and enjoy the family time. Two weeks after his brother was born, Gray actually had a great idea, he asked me when we were going to return Reid to the hospital, which I suppose is always an available option to reduce your stress.

Already conflicted about my identity and my available options, I also knew that my plan needed to be tempered with some reality. Admittedly when I had children, I had the freedom to quit my job. Unfortunately, I had a list of "must do's" lodged in my head, and I wanted my children (as I want you) to have the best possible stack of pancakes. What did that consist of? Material things like a private education, a huge house, and the extras that other students think everyone else has; or intangibles like time with me, fun activities, family and friends. Being mindful and aware of your values comes in very handy when you are faced with these choices. I realize now how relatively unaware I was when I had my *pajama moment*.

My Pajama Moment

When Reid became old enough to sort of communicate, he came into the kitchen in the morning and always had a minor meltdown if he found me in a bathrobe. He cried, "Put your nightball (nightgown) on!" He obviously was more perceptive at two than I was at thirty-something because it took me a while to understand his nightgown fetish. It turns out that he had observed that on work days when he awoke, I showered and was in a robe before donning my business suit, but on my days off, I lingered in my jammies. I can still hear him screaming as I left the house for work, and I essentially cried half of the way to the office. Of course, he was back inside happily unraveling rolls of toilet paper across the house when I reached my destination, but I was overcome with guilt and anxiety.

There is no one-size-fits-all answer or anything magical that you should do as a working parent. The period of time after children come along represents a life transition, and you need to handle it accordingly. Spend some time in the blender stage; break out your cognitive behavioral therapy, relaxation techniques, cinematherapy, bibilotherapy, humor, and self-exploration tools. Please don't be afraid to ask for help, seek support, or lean on others. Take care of yourself because if you don't, then how will you be able to take care of anyone else? Listen to your body, be mindful, and pay attention to yourself. This is an exhausting time, but it can also be a fabulous opportunity to start your next pancake. Armed with all that you have learned, I promise you can do it.

Take a cue from Donna, for example, who worked for eleven years in a marketing job before having a child. She found herself very torn between work and family within her son's first year and decided to quit her job. After a couple of years at home, she found herself bored and started to work part-time at her husband's business, which she is still doing. She has found an appropriate balance based on her value system.

Judy, by contrast, is a lawyer who worked hard to make partner in her firm. She took family leave for three months when each of her two children was born but is very comfortable working full-time and enjoys the help of in-home nanny care for her children. She almost lost her mind during the family leave periods and feels that she needs to work outside of the home to maintain her sanity, financial position, sense of self-worth, and overall life satisfaction.

Laura worked outside of the home as a dental hygienist. She worked full-time when her first child was born, cut back to part-time with her second child, and quit altogether when her third came along. She feels very fulfilled (and definitely not bored) as a full-time homemaker; in fact, she feels very fortunate to be able to stay home without incurring financial strain.

I have several more examples of women who have made choices like these, and I am confident that you do, too, hopefully success stories of those who have made happy choices for themselves. When you decide what you want, ask for it. And don't be shy. Be creative and confident in putting yourself and your children first. When making your decision, please remember to ask yourself whether your choices are as congruent with your values as they could possibly be.

Empty Kitchen

One day, I was explaining to a friend about how bittersweet it was to see my sons grow up and become independent. On the one hand, according to John Rosemond, an expert in family psychology and a renowned author and speaker on parenting, the foremost job of a parent is to raise the child to become independent. Therefore, when my sons ask me to wait in the car after I chauffeur them somewhere, I'm proud that I have done a marvelous job raising them to live without me. On the other hand, it is mildly hurtful to accept that they would die if any of their friends actually laid eyes on me.

I liken being a parent to being a best man or maid of honor in a wedding party. we all have been there. The bride instructed me to wear this ugly dress that was such a putrid color that no company manufactured shoes to match. So I bought plain shoes and had them dyed that exact shade, knowing full well that I would never wear them again. Naturally, I shopped for said shoes, traveled to the wedding at my own expense, and waited on the bride the day before the ceremony, so that she could completely ignore me all day except for when she handed me her bouquet during the vow exchange.

Why did I do all of this? Because I care about her a great deal and, therefore, wanted to help make her day special. I knew that she appreciated what I did for her, even though understandably she didn't have time to express her thanks directly to me. This knowledge was my reward, so that while the experience was somewhat thankless, it simultaneously was richly rewarding.

Remember this when your children leave home for whatever reason. They are grateful for all that you have done, even if, like the bride, they do not express their thanks. I can't tell you how many women have shared with me how justifiably difficult it is to undergo this transition.

Corinne led a harried, hectic life as a single parent for twenty years while raising two sons and working as a full-time data processor. She is legitimately proud of the fact that both of her sons are now thriving in their own right: one has joined the Navy, and the other is currently working his way through college. Although she works full-time, she feels that something is missing in her life. To combat her instinct to isolate herself, stay in her bathrobe, and watch movies all day, she actually has taken a second job to keep herself busy and distracted.

Similarly, Sarah's third child just left the home to attend college, and although she misses her three boys, she is delighted to have more time for herself. She got a new puppy, became more active in her church, started walking daily with a female friend, and joined a book club. Her husband is still employed, but she looks forward to his retirement so that they can travel together (and not just to see their children).

This transition is unsettling whether or not you have worked outside of the home, although this may be harder for nonworking women in terms of available time. Either way, you have devoted a tremendous amount of time, thought, emotion, and energy to your children. Now that they are gone, you feel a void and yearn to fill it. Is it your calendar, your heart, your soul, or your laundry basket that is empty? Do yourself a favor and take care of yourself. Figure out how to fill the void and begin your exciting new pancake. Try to think of the positive like you have been a good parent, you have made a difference in someone's life, and you can actually use your own telephone without waiting, listen to the music *you* like in your vehicle, or maybe even buy a real car now that you have lost that chauffeur feeling.

It isn't exactly a surprise that they left. You have known for several years that they would leave, just as you knew they would arrive in about forty weeks. Plan ahead, and pack your bags along with theirs. For example, I have informed Gray and Reid that they will have to attend a college with a PhD program in psychology, so that I will be able to go with them. (If you have not seen *Back to School* starring Rodney Dangerfield, kindly add it to your cinematherapy list.) But that's just my solution, and I am confident that you will find yours.

There is also a recent and growing trend for children to return home, the "boomerang" generation that has followed the "baby boom". So, take comfort as you weep over their departure, as your empty nest may turn cluttered or even crowded down the road (especially if you downsize after they first leave). Their future return might really make you crazy because they are effectively grown-up houseguests on whom you have to wait hand and foot.

Pass the Hor-Moans

Finally, other life transitions that women have the privilege of experiencing, of course, are those lovely hormone-induced ones. Given that I'm an expert in the emotional rather than the medical side of menopause, I will steer clear of a technical explanation of this topic—except to point out that it is understandable to feel a little off when something you have experienced once a month for about thirty-eight years (a total of 456 times) stops. That's one heck of an ending, especially when it involves chemicals that affect your mood. Definitely allow yourself to take two Advil and call me in the morning. And it's not just the end of your monthly cycle but rather the end of an era during which you had an identity as a woman with the ability to be reproductive as well as productive. This transition, like any other, thus involves a loss, an ending which has to be processed. For the men, try to imagine suddenly not being able to experience something that you have done 456 times, for example holding the remote, leaving the seat up, not asking for directions when lost, or any other activity that impacts your mood.

If you would like to read more about women's issues, I refer you to the Recommended Resource list for further reading. I sincerely hope that some male readers turn there in the interest of bolstering your emotional intelligence regarding the unique transition issues women face.

The Flip

After the blender stage, it is time to think about your next pancake. You begin to let go of the emotions surrounding whatever event precipitated your transition, accept what has happened, and think about your future. You're getting ready to make a new pancake and strike gold. Some may get to this stage in a matter of days, while for others it takes months. Limited resources and support systems, underdeveloped coping mechanisms, inexperience in dealing effectively with stressful events, and multiple stressors can prolong the pancake process. In my case, nineteen years at the same financial institution was a long time, almost half my life. I was naïve to think that I would just forget about it overnight. It's like longtime cigarette smokers, who puff away for decades, think that they can quit cold turkey, and completely forget that they ever smoked. That certainly isn't the norm even if you plaster your entire body with nicotine patches. I was inexperienced at coping with loss when I was suddenly faced with two at once, but I was lucky to have financial and social support to weather the storm.

As you begin to let go of the old, you gradually begin to think about the new, "That chapter of my life is over; I wonder what the next one will bring?" or, "That relationship has ended, but I know that a new one will come along at the right time." You've disposed of that first imperfect pancake, so how can you move on to tastier ones? Some of the negative thoughts and feelings that you were experiencing in the blender stage are replaced with more hopeful, energetic, optimistic ones. The past is behind you, but the future that lies ahead is a bit blurred and uncertain, and it's time to start adjusting the focus.

For some, a cathartic or defining moment jump-starts the next pancake, and some cognitive reframing begins. My flip probably occurred toward the end of that first summer when Gray and Reid were getting ready to go back to school. It was a bit of a throwback to my own childhood—that feeling that summer is coming to a close, and it's time to buy new clothes, supplies, and the pièce de résistance, the lunchbox. Actually, reality hit me like a brick, "Holy smokes, my kids aren't going to be around, and what am I going to do with me, myself, and I all day?" Come to think of it, except for vacations, this was the first time in my life since pre-kindergarten that I was neither a student, nor a worker bee. It was time to let go of the past and look forward.

During this part of the transition journey, it's great if you can lose your baggage and move on. I am aware of the "you take your baggage with you" cliché, but please don't. If you have to enlist the help of an airline, coach or therapist to lose your baggage, that's okay—just do whatever it takes.

Here's how one of my clients experienced "letting go". Joan was married for five years when her husband had several affairs. Adopted at birth, she had a lifelong challenge coping with events that smacked of rejection. Given this profile, her husband's betrayal devastated her. She cycled through shock, despair, and anger, and these emotions initially crippled her. She doubted her ability to move on in life without further rejection. Joan leaned heavily on her support network and additionally sought counseling. She was unable to release her feelings toward her husband for several months, and they maintained a highly argumentative relationship because her hurt and anger frequently flared up. Joan eventually let go of her feelings when she realized that her high-conflict marriage was detrimental to their children. This revelation was her defining moment, and she was able move forward toward a more peaceful and warm family environment.

The Perfect Pancake

If you have been able to dispose of that first not-so-hot pancake, you can now start fresh and go for the solid golden one. This process feels a bit like when you are ready for a new vehicle and you begin to test-drive various models to find the ideal one for you. For me, my children's return to school in the fall provoked a surge of energy and a call to thought and action. I was thinking about transferring my skills to a different industry when I received a chance call from a headhunter. He was trying to fill the executive director position at the local symphony, which was six years old and on its third director. In spite of the fact that I'm completely tone deaf (and you *definitely* don't want to hear me sing), I got very energized at this prospect. The previous directors were music gurus who didn't understand the business side. Now, they wanted someone with a command of business but who didn't necessarily understand the difference between a trumpet and cornet. They ended up finding someone with a superior mastery of both arts, but nonetheless the idea of making such a drastic change inspired me to explore other fields.

And then I had another idea. I didn't want to follow my parents and older brother into teaching, which I had rebelled against in my first adult transition from college to the work world. And so I became a student. I registered for an undergraduate abnormal psychology class at the local public university and started school when my sons did. The boys were so wonderfully supportive of my plan and curious about the subject, my homework, and my grades. It was very rewarding to have two such fine young men standing behind me, and to be able to compare notes on our school days. I fell in love with the world of psychology and decided to take the prerequisites and apply for the masters in counseling psychology program.

In spite of that decision, I still was testing the waters. During that fall, I volunteered as a teacher's aide at a shelter for battered women. The teacher with whom I had the privilege of working was dynamite and wowed with me her enthusiasm for what she did and her ability to be simultaneously tough and nurturing. She was born to teach in this setting and had previously worked in detention centers for juvenile women. (Don't you just hate people that find their calling early on? We'll get to some ideas about how to do that in just a bit.) This teaching experience taught me that I sincerely enjoyed being around children and that I'm passionate about the helping professions but that I would prefer to help others in a capacity other than that of a teacher. I thought that the counseling role would be a way for me to have my pancake and eat it too.

Many of my former bank colleagues tested the waters as well. For example, a former corporate banker I know enjoyed a sabbatical, during which he tried out various business investments (like a furniture business, real estate, and financial management), before deciding to purchase a restaurant franchise option and opening the first location in our city. A human resources professional I knew could never find the perfect beach chair and so she invented one and had it patented. A couple of others wrote a book. Naturally not as good as this one, but at least these bankers-turned-authors tested the waters. These individuals had let go of their previous positions and were now trying new ones on for size.

Similarly, a client named Claire lost her house to a fire started by holiday candles placed too close to a decorated tree. The loss of the place she had called home for so long and her belongings therein, including photographs of her grown children, devastated her. For a while, she stayed with friends, immobilized by her shock and sadness. Once she was able to let go of her emotions, she started to explore alternative places to live. She actually ended up in a much smaller condominium, which required less maintenance but had plenty of good neighbors. Her willingness to test new waters allowed her to find a positive solution.

Self-Exploration

Expanding your horizons often leads to a deeper exploration of self. You start by looking around your environment but then turn inward to examine yourself. Once I started the psychology program, I began my more profound self-exploration, an attempt to get in closer touch with my values, strengths, interests, abilities, preferences, and desires, tempered with the financial reality of raising two children and, one day, retiring. Unlike the teacher I just described, I don't think that in forty-three years I had found my calling or taken the time to conduct a search for meaning in anything other than a superficial way. For the first time, I had stepped off the treadmill of the daily grind or at least set it on pause mode. Up to this point, I had gone with my gut for career decisions and, to some extent, personal choices. In certain respects, this strategy had paid off; however, I honestly never felt like my professional life had real meaning. I had accepted my first pancake as the status quo and never stopped to try my hand at making better ones. I needed to define or refine my self-concept and view of the world.

Many times, in fact, I suffered from the impostor syndrome, where you believe that people who think highly of you don't see that you are actually much less competent than you appear to be—you are a fake. (I hope that you are thinking what I am thinking, that this would be a great time to invest in some CBT.) For example, during my last couple of years at Bank of America, my boss asked me to speak at a stock analyst conference in New York with five hundred attendees. There was one other female speaker during the three-day conference, and all the other speakers were CEOs of Fortune 100 corporations. Of course, I thought my boss had either completely lost his mind or erroneously sent the memo to me. I actually called him to point out his error in the most diplomatic way I could find, but he explained why I was the perfect person from his perspective. The moral of this tale is that while there were many things about my years in banking that I have enjoyed, I always felt a bit like a fish out of water, that I didn't belong, and that I should have been doing something else.

I don't think that I'm the only person who has ever felt like an impostor.

A client of mine named Karen shared with me that her work in pharmaceutical sales was lucrative but not rewarding. She had been a top performer in her division, but she didn't feel like a star. Dressed to the nines and calling on doctors all day looked impressive to others but left Karen feeling empty. Through some self-exploration, she realized that she felt more at home with patients than physicians. She decided to go back to school for patient care in spite of the smaller financial reward.

Dr. Albert Ellis coined a terrific, albeit a little crass, term, "musturbation", which refers to those should, must, or ought to inner statements that make you feel guilty, inadequate, or just plain bad. Although a successful businesswoman, my internal voice said that I *should* be something else—a teacher like my parents and older brother. I felt like I *ought* to do something different.

Do you ever feel like a fake, misfit, or must-fit? If so, I encourage you to heed this wake-up call. It is alerting you not to settle for this pancake but to create a more fulfilling one. You don't have to live by the musts within; in fact you really should define your own. If you know others that are living a lie, help them find their way back to authenticity as well.

"By the time a man realizes that maybe his father was right, he usually has a son who thinks he's wrong."
—Charles Wadsworth

Based on my own experience, I have come to realize how important self-examination is, and so I am going to spend some time on this stage. Psychologist Erik Erikson's work on psychosocial development over the lifespan is nothing short of brilliant and true to life. Erikson's core idea is that we all pass through eight development stages between infancy and adulthood. Each stage presents challenges, which if not mastered will resurface as problems in the future. Erikson's fifth developmental stage is identity versus identity confusion, which occurs during adolescence (from ages ten to twenty). During this period we attempt to find out who we are, what our values are, and where we are headed in life.

Adolescents are exposed to a host of adult concepts, like various careers, hobbies, romantic relationships, sexual activities, and financial scenarios. Parents must allow the adolescent to explore alternative paths in an independent and inquisitive manner, so that they can achieve a healthy identity. Identity confusion will occur if the parents try to choose an identity for their child or don't allow the child enough freedom to explore. It's okay to impose a reasonable curfew, but by all means, let the adolescent out to see the world. Be there to offer information, guidance, love, and support, but let the emerging scientists explore because they just might discover something truly great. It's certainly fair to say that I left adolescence with a somewhat dazed, confused, or not quite baked identity. I knew that my parents thought that I should be a teacher, but I had not yet clarified my own vision for my life. I believe that I was in touch with what others wanted for me but not want I wanted for myself.

Again, I don't think I'm the first person in the world who felt pressure from parents and/or others to do something that went against your own grain.

A client named Gary came from a long line of physicians. His grandfather and father were both cardiologists, and his two uncles were family practice doctors. His older brother was branching out and going to dental school. Guess what Gary wanted to do? Deliver babies? Deliver speeches? Deliver mail? No, he wanted to deliver the most delicious cuisine he could. He wanted to attend culinary school and become a chef even though he felt like he should want to go to medical school.

It's okay if your identity isn't rigidly cast during adolescence because actually your personal identity can change over time as you change roles and your values shift accordingly. A core component of Donald Super's lifespan theory is *self-concept*, which is the way individuals see themselves and the world around them. Biological characteristics, social roles, and social interactions shape your self-concept. Super acknowledges that most adults re-evaluate their career plans at several points during their lifetime. They recycle back through an exploration of themselves and shape a new path. It actually is a privilege to be able to recycle and have a second (or third, fourth, or fifth) chance to find your calling. And remember, your career is what you do and not who you are. If and when you get fired, remember that you are still the same person; you just aren't doing the same job any longer.

"Getting fired is nature's way of telling you that you had the wrong job in the first place."
—Hal Lancaster

For me, the start down the psycho-(wait, there's more)-therapist path precipitated my recycling. As I was finishing up the prerequisites, beginning the actual graduate classes, and being a mother, I also was second-guessing myself every step of the way. On the verge of committing to the graduate program, I was wrestling with whether to continue down this new road or turn back down the more lucrative and familiar world of business. A friend wanted me to do business development work for her executive search company because she and her partner needed to build their client base. I helped out long enough to realize that I wanted to go forward and not back. It must have been the panty hose or something because she and her partner were great co-workers.

Tonya, a client of mine, worked in health care administration before she embarked on a recycling period. During this time, she had three children, and daily life became more and more hectic and less and less enjoyable. She had always felt like she ought to work, but the thrill was gone. She initially cut back to part time, but this reduced her pay and not her output. She thought about what could give her more satisfaction and decided to work at her church. This change allowed her to express her faith through serving others; it also provided a more flexible schedule conducive to spending more time with her children. From time to time, she questioned her move, but for that time of her life, it was a tasty pancake.

Self-Discovery

"The first step to getting the thing you want
out of this life is deciding what you want."
—Ben Stein

I don't mean to suggest that you need to run off and study psychology to reshape your identity. I'm simply proposing that soul-searching, self-examination, and self-questioning are viable ways to conduct your own investigation and that the fruits of these labors are delicious and delightful.

Okay, so how do you decide what you want? How do you figure out what makes you tick? What are your passions, your pleasures, and your purpose? How do you make a prettier pancake? It's so easy that it hurts. You need to become mindful, which means "paying attention in a particular way: on purpose, in the present moment, and nonjudgmentally" (Kabat-Zinn, p.4). It's the opposite of being mindless or absent-minded. Being mindless or absent is when you are in the middle of a sentence and completely forget what you are talking about. Or you drive to the wrong place, do not rememeber a word of what you just read, or what somebody just said.

Sock-et to Me

One of my most memorable absent moments was my ninth grade biology class on the day we were dissecting frogs (yuck!). The teacher was droning on about I don't remember what, but I'm guessing it was about amphibians or something. I was spacing out. In this state, I managed to stick a pair of metal tweezers into a live electrical socket at the lab table where I was seated. Sparks flew, I had little black spots on my face, and tiny holes appeared in my dreaded panty hose. Of course, I tried to act cool, calm, and collected as though nothing had happened. Unfortunately, my lab partner started to bust out laughing, and soon, others caught on to my shocking act.

In any event, rather than jolting yourself to wisdom by darn near electrocuting yourself, become mindful by a) learning how and b) practicing. The easiest way is to pay attention to how you feel while performing a given day-to-day activity. For most people, eating is a mindless activity, especially in today's "Supersize me!" society. Think about people at the movies who sit in the dark stuffing kernel after kernel of popcorn or piece after piece of candy in their mouths without really even tasting the stuff (I can't bring myself to call it food). An alternative way to eat (and to stay slimmer) is to slow down and enjoy the food bite by bite, flavor by flavor, and taste by taste.

"Wherever you go, there you are."
—Jon Kabat-Zinn

Mindfulness means that you are being aware of the present moment. You aren't judging, reflecting, or thinking, but you're observing. You're there with the sole purpose of paying attention on purpose in the present moment. Being mindful requires an increased awareness of all aspects of self, including mind, body, heart, and soul. Mindfulness is an intentional focused awareness. It offers a way to take charge of your life and to cope with stress, pain, illness, and challenges of life, such as *life transitions*.

The University of Massachusetts Medical School houses the Center for Mindfulness in Medicine, Health Care, and Society (CFM), which was founded in 1995 but originated in 1979 with Jon Kabat-Zinn's Stress Reduction Clinic. The stress reduction program boasts more than 13,000 graduates of its eight-week program. Those who completed the program report their results, including an increased ability to relax, greater energy/ enthusiasm for life, and an ability to cope more effectively with stressful situations. The following exercises hit the highlights of information covered during the eight weeks.

Kabat-Zinn developed a wonderful mindfulness exercise called the raisin exercise which forces one to eat a single raisin very slowly and with acute awareness. I'm going to use another derivative of the grape—champagne—to illustrate how to drink mindfully. I truly enjoy champagne, and because it's so darned expensive, you should sip it really slowly, savoring it, or you will be broke. (Please feel free to substitute any type of bubbly beverage like club soda, regular soda, or even caffeine-free, low-carb, no-sugar, no-fat, diet soda.)

> "Come quickly, I am tasting stars!"
> —Dom Perignon

Champagne Brain

- Remove the chilled bottle from the fridge and look at it. (Pause.)
- Take your favorite flute out of the cupboard and place it near the bottle. (Breathe.)
- Pay attention to the label. (Pause.)
- Think about the name of the brand. (Breathe.)
- Try to picture what the vineyard looks like. Is it in France, California, or Spain? Is it hilly, flat, big, or small? (Pause.)
- Imagine what the grapes looked like before they were processed, when the sunlight hit them, or when they were wet with dew or rain. (Breathe.)
- Observe the beautiful glass and think about why it has its unique shape. (Pause.)
- Now, slowly pour a reasonable amount of the beverage into the flute. (Breathe.)
- Watch how it settles into the glass before the bubbles start to float upward and until a tiny layer of froth finally forms at the top. (Pause.)
- Be mesmerized by those bubbles in the moment. (Breathe.)
- Now, raise the glass and pay attention to how it feels.

(Pause.)
- Bring it toward your lips slowly enough that you smell the bouquet before the liquid hits your taste buds. (Breathe.)
- Breathe in that fragrance and imagine how it will taste. (Pause.)
- Finally, close your eyes and take a sip small enough to savor but big enough to taste. (Breathe.)
- As you swallow, picture the sun setting on the vineyard. (Pause.)
- Pay attention to how the liquid feels as it travels down your throat. (Breathe.)
- Notice how the taste still lingers on your tongue. (Pause.)
- Set the glass back down, and watch what happens to those bubbles. (Breathe.)
- Stay present in the moment, and enjoy a few more deep abdominal breaths.

Repeat as necessary, and if you overdo it, take two Advil and call me in the morning. I'm confident that you'll appreciate the benefit of taking time out to pause and to think about what you are doing and how it makes you feel. You should repeat this activity again until it becomes a skill, because it can be learned.

Sitting Mindfully

Another exercise to help you develop your mindfulness is to practice while sitting.

- Find and enjoy a comfortable sitting position. This can be on the floor, a mat, or a pillow.
- Focus your attention on the peaceful rise and fall of your breath.
- Center your mind on the feelings as you inhale and exhale and on the sensations as your breath enters your nose or mouth and as it fills your lungs and diaphragm.
- If your mind drifts off, pull your attention back to your breath.
- Should you become distracted by thoughts, acknowledge

them and return to the present moment.
- Create more inner peace by detaching from your thoughts. You can achieve this by labeling them as you dismiss them. For example, "Worry," you tell yourself, "please go away, I'll catch up with you later."

Please spend at least twenty but preferably thirty minutes in this state.

Mindfulness To Go

- If at all possible, go outside to a serene location. Wear comfortable shoes so you can walk.
- Stretch out your legs and pay attention to the release of tension in your muscles.
- Repeat the stretches, but this time, work your neck and spine.
- Begin to walk by concentrating on your breathing. After a few deep breaths, begin to count how many steps you take as you inhale and exhale.
- Think only about how your body is feeling as it moves. Feel your feet as they strike the ground: heel, ball, toe; heel, ball, toe. Notice the rhythm of your steps.
- Be aware of how your legs and hips move as you stride and how your arms glide along in counterpoint to your legs.
- Notice the core of your body below your navel and how all of your movement flows from this source in harmony.
- Now, expand your awareness to include the environment that surrounds you. Take it in—whether it's the roar of the waves, the sound of a stream, the call of a bird, or the blow of a horn.

This exercise can be adapted to an indoor setting as well. Even a treadmill in a crowded gym will suffice. In fact, you are commended if you can get into your zone in an environment less conducive to inner peace.

Heart Smarts

I am not alone in my thinking that chronological age matters about as much as academic IQ when it comes to life satisfaction. Just ask Daniel Goleman, a prolific researcher, writer, professor, and speaker about what he terms as *emotional intelligence*. After I read his brilliant book, *Emotional Intelligence: Why It Can Matter More Than IQ*, I immediately became the CEO of his fan club, although I envy his creative genius for coining the phrase *emotional hijacking*. (Don't you love that term?) It refers to those times that you kind of lose it and unload on your boss, partner, child, or dog. If you are human, you know precisely what I'm saying. Due to some fascinating brain chemistry, your emotions can hijack your reason but can be better regulated by honing your emotional intelligence.

Even though he earned a PhD from Harvard and subsequently taught there, Goleman is anything but a nerd. In fact, his basic premise is that academic IQ actually accounts for at the most 20 percent of your satisfaction and success in life. (Thank God for small blessings.) If my math is right, that means that 80 percent of your life satisfaction depends on your emotional intelligence. That makes it a hugely important ingredient in your perfect pancake recipe. Dr. Goleman studied a group of Harvard students over a long period of time and found that in middle age the men with the highest college test scores did *not* enjoy higher professional success (like salary, prestige, or productivity) or personal life satisfaction (like family, friendships, or romance) than their lower-scoring peers did. There are several other subsequent studies that support the same premise. Academic IQ isn't the best indicator of success and satisfaction in life. What historically has been taught in schools (like dissecting frogs) doesn't necessarily prepare one for a fulfilling life.

A superior predictor of life success and happiness is emotional intelligence. The following list includes different areas that make up your emotional intelligence.

- Self-awareness, which is knowing yourself and recognizing a feeling when it occurs. This is the *mindfulness* idea rearing its

pretty head again.
- Emotional control, which is regulating your mood and controlling yourself. For example, not lambasting your boss, spouse, or dog, but instead practicing CBT, relaxation exercises, restraint, or whatever techniques work for you.
- Self-motivation, which is getting into the flow and delaying gratification in the interest of productivity. This is like the athlete running twenty-six miles to earn a banana.
- Empathy, which is being attuned to the needs and wants of others, *the* critical people skill. Empathic people succeed in fields like the helping professions, sales, or management.
- Relationships, which are interactions with and management of the emotions of others or basically getting along well with others. High interpersonal effectiveness breeds leaders, social butterflies, and the cool kids of the environment.

According to Goleman, these are the skills that help individuals achieve happiness and success during their lives. And that's not even the good news. I called these items *skills* intentionally because skills (like cognitive behavioral techniques, relaxation, and mindfulness) can be learned. Therefore, if you feel down because you think you're deficient in any one of these areas, cheer up. You can acquire these skills. During a life transition is an ideal time to learn these new skills, should you decide that it would benefit you. (If you even give this consideration, I promise I will update a skill of my own, technology, which I desperately want to do. For example, I don't own a Blackberry, blueberry, or raspberry, but I'm seriously considering acquiring one to top off my new pancake or at least to bury the first one.)

Although it's never too late to acquire emotional intelligence, I strongly advocate schooling your emotions early on. Our schools should focus more on what will make our children happy and successful, namely emotional intelligence. Had I listened to my parents and become an academic, I would have instituted the following daily schedule for elementary school. The same type of exercise also can be adapted to home or workplace settings.

sCool Day

- First Period: Share how you really are feeling today. (Come on, dig deep, and be honest.)
- Second Period: Sit next to a person you intensely dislike (probably someone of the opposite gender) and practice getting along for fifteen minutes.
- Third Period: Engage in physical activity (not fighting with the person from restraint exercise in second period but blowing off some steam or extra energy).
- Fourth Period: Do some creative work but make sure it's something you enjoy (because you're self-motivated and energized from the physical activity and will uncover your talents during this free time).
- Fifth Period: Eat lunch mindfully. (Your brain and tummy now are depleted so fuel them.)
- Sixth Period: Talk to all of your classmates and build your interpersonal effectiveness. Give a speech and boost your leadership skills/popularity. Get along with everyone and appreciate the diversity of the class, even the girls.
- Seventh Period: Briefly cover all of the stuff that you'll have to answer on the SATs (if you don't Christmas-tree the answer sheet) in case anyone actually still cares about academic IQ if and when you apply to college.
- Dismissal: Listen for bell, and rush out to share great stories with whoever is there for you. Talk with the bus driver, or better yet the biggest geek on the bus.

Based on this proposal, I probably don't have to tell you how happy I was the day Gray and Reid brought home their "feelings cube," which they had made in guidance class. Of course, I could hardly make out the words given their "needs improvement" handwriting. It was a cardboard die with emotions listed on each face (like anger, embarrassment, sadness, happiness, and so on). They explained to me that each student had to take turns rolling the die and describe a time when they had experienced the relevant emotion. Naturally, my boys thought this was stupid and annoying, and, of course, I thought it was a sign that our school system one day might catch on to the value of emotional intelligence. Unfortunately, it's probably just my learned cognitive behavioral therapy and positive psychology optimism kicking in.

Clearly I don't intend to belittle the value of traditional intelligence; in fact, smart people energize me, and, like Goleman, I went to Harvard for one of three degrees. Even Goleman admits that IQ is as important as one business day. Smarts are advantageous (and it's too bad they aren't also contagious when you interact with that dork on the bus ride home from school). The best thing about having a high IQ is that learning emotional intelligence is probably easier for you, so you will have more free time to invent something brilliant that will benefit the rest of us. If you would like to assess or develop your own emotional intelligence, please refer to the Recommended Resources list in the appendices for some relevant and useful tools.

The Pancake Principle

"Happiness is that state of consciousness which
proceeds from the achievement of one's values."
—Ayn Rand

Once you are more self-aware and know what you want to
achieve, how do you maximize the opportunity that a transition
period presents? How do you combine the best ingredients for
a more perfect pancake? First and foremost, you need to figure
out your values and priorities—or simply stated, your personal
philosophy. Values represent your core inner guide for how you
want to live. If you understand what is valuable or important to
you, your direction in life follows that understanding. Although
during adolescence you strive to shape your own identity and
rebel against your parents, after you mature, 80 percent of your
values match those of your parents. Later in life, it's beneficial
to revisit these values when your role has changed and you have
distanced yourself from adolescence.

And how do you figure out your values during self-exploration?
This is really easy. Simply pretend that you'll drop dead in three
months and decide what you want to do between now and then.
I'm serious. Your choices of how to spend those last few days will
tell you a lot about what is truly important to you. Would you
surround yourself with family and friends, travel the globe, get
your affairs in order, have an affair, or just finish this book?

I shouldn't make light of such a solemn subject, but existential
exercises of this nature are extremely insightful, and I *strongly*

recommend them. Accordingly I suggest reading *The Myth of Tomorrow: Seven Essential Keys for Living the Life You Want* by Dr. Gary Buffone. Although it's perhaps somewhat morbid, deciding how to spend today in case your life ends tomorrow is thought provoking. Please don't wait for a wake-up call to understand your values because you won't maximize the time between now and then, which saddens me. Time and money share the same downside because they can't be spent twice.

If planning the last weeks of your life is too simple (or too depressing) for you, there are a host of other tools to help you uncover *your* values. There are many values clarification exercises out there, including the Valuable Exercise that follows this paragraph. These lists are a bit like the NFL season, wherein you start with thirty-two teams, cut them down to eight, and then finally knock it down to two. Please don't just take your pencil and madly circle words. Practice your relaxation skills. Close your eyes, take a few deep breaths, pause, and think about what's important to *you*. Repeat: important to *you*. For example, if you select concern for others, fine, but I hope you don't make your choice for the wrong reason (for example, because you think you will be less liked if you don't choose it). If you really value status or success, it's okay; you're an adult now and can make your own choices. Your values are what *you* treasure and not what you or someone else thinks they ought to be. Your values aren't static or fixed for life. Your values can shift over time, and you need to be mindful of them and prepared to rework your lifestyle accordingly. For example, becoming a parent altered my values in a pretty drastic manner. Many other men and women have had the same experience.

"Most people are other people. Their thoughts are someone else's opinions, their lives a mimicry, their passions a quotation."
—Oscar Wilde

Valuable Exercise

Please begin by circling no more than fifteen values, then take a deep breath, and review your choices. If you wish to add values other than those on this list, please feel free to do so. This list is just a guide, not gospel. Now eliminate at least five of the fifteen, leaving no more than ten core values. Finally, revisit your choices, and eliminate five more, leaving only five. Take a few deep breaths, relax, and make sure that these are the things that *you* value above all. Then you can start to think about whether or not the way you spend your time is congruent with this top five.

Common Personal Values
  Accomplishment
  Accountability
  Adventure
  Beauty
  Concern for Others
  Continuous Improvement
  Cooperation
  Creativity
  Decisiveness
  Democracy
  Equality
  Faith
  Freedom
  Gratitude
  Hard Work
  Harmony
  Honesty
  Honor
  Independence
  Integrity
  Justice
  Knowledge
  Leadership
  Love
  Loyalty

Meaning
Money
Peace
Perfection
Personal Growth
Prosperity
Respect for Others
Security
Service
Stability
Status
Success
Teamwork
Timeliness
Tradition
Tranquility
Trust
Truth
Unity
Variety
Wisdom

Should you prefer to try an online exercise of this nature, kindly refer to Weiler, Nicholas, www.career.test.biz

Bring on the Bacon

Once you understand your values (at least at this point of your current life transition), you need to get in touch with your strengths. Marcus Buckingham and Donald O. Clifton point out the historical error of our ways in their outstanding work *Now, Discover Your Strengths*. They demonstrate that we have had it backward in our society; we talk about fixing our weaknesses rather than building up our strengths. During the latter part of my banking career, I was included in what the organization called *talent planning*. If your boss identified you as high potential or high professional, you would create a development plan and work on your development areas (also known as your weaknesses). Talent planning can be a very valuable activity; however, the focus should be maximizing your strengths and managing around your weaknesses rather than fixing your flaws. It's no different at my children's schools, where the parent-teacher feedback revolves around areas for improvement and development needs rather than ways to build on innate strengths that will help them succeed.

According to Buckingham and Clifton, the ingredients for strengths are talent, knowledge, and skills. The way to maximize your strengths is to identify your innate abilities and build on them with knowledge and skills. All of the time, you hear people say, "He's a *natural* athlete," "She's a *born* actress," or "He has been a charmer from *day one*." These qualities are talents, and they were there when you were born and will stay with you as you grow older. They are consistent, enduring positive or negative traits that you can apply beneficially.

By way of illustration, I'm a natural athlete, and I enjoy a variety of sports because I am good at them. By contrast, I'm a domestic disaster in every room of my house but the kitchen because I love to cook (except with a blender). I think my cooking craze started when I had those high-level strategic jobs and the fruits of my labor took months to come to fruition. You see, unlike my strategies, baked goods were tangible within minutes (if I didn't eat all of the dough). I'm hopelessly bad at interior decorating. Our house looks like we just moved in yesterday, except that I have managed to throw out the boxes. When I worked a traditional full-time schedule, I told myself that I was too busy to decorate. But now, I confess the real reason—I have zero talent in this arena; therefore, I don't enjoy it because incompetence doesn't feel good. I don't get passionate about choosing fabric for drapes; in fact, I would rather have all of my teeth drilled without Novocain.

The most effective way to identify your talents is—again—to pay attention to yourself, especially to your gut, off-the-top-of-your-head reactions to events. (We touched on this earlier in the discussion of CBT.) Hopefully, you've practiced your self-awareness so extensively that you immediately know what kinds of behaviors come naturally to you.

In addition, consider your passions, which originate early in life from your brain's synaptic activity, and develop based on genetics and experience. If during childhood you found yourself drawn to certain activities and turned off by others, then these may be signs of talents. An incorrigible tomboy, I literally never played with dolls and always longed to be outdoors. Shopping for clothes (especially bathing suits), by contrast, was torture for me, and to this day, I believe that prisoners should have to serve some of their sentences at the mall. (That might actually help with the overcrowding of our prisons.) I can't tell you how grateful I was for the advent of catalog and Internet shopping. In my youth, I wanted to play volleyball, figure-skate, and be in the company of others. I got my energy from physical activity and interacting with others. These were my hankerings and still are. What are yours?

An effective way to uncover your own longings is to create your personal "I'd rather be ..." bumper sticker. (Okay, I know that "My child is an honor student at ..." and "I'd rather be fishing" are probably tied for most irritating.) My favorite bumper sticker is "Life is a gift, that's why it's called the present." Think about what you would rather be doing in the present with this gift called life.

In addition, pleasure is a great indicator of talent. If you enjoy doing something, it's in large part because you are good at it, and if you are good at doing something, you will enjoy doing it. Go ahead and check it out. Usually you can learn these pleasurable activities more quickly than others. If, for example, you learn to snowboard with relative ease (or at least without breaking your wrist as I did), you probably have a talent for it and related sports.

> **"Knowledge is of two kinds. We know a subject**
> **ourselves, or we find information on it."**
> —Samuel Johnson

Knowledge and skills, by contrast, aren't innate, but the good news is they can be learned (like cognitive behavioral therapy, relaxation, and mindfulness). There are two types of knowledge, factual (content) and experiential (real life) knowledge. Skills are the steps you follow when performing an activity like blending, stirring, pouring, flipping, and serving to make pancakes. Again, what better time to acquire new knowledge and skills than while making your new perfect pancake, particularly if you intend to change your life's course after completing your self-discovery?

Kitchen Helpers

If you're having trouble getting in touch with your inner voice, even after practicing relaxation, mindfulness, and emotional intelligence, it's okay. There are many kitchen helpers out there to assist you in making the perfect pancake. There's no shame in getting help with your pancake preparation; after all, some people even have their own personal chef.

Objective input from assessments can supplement your own introspection, validate your self-perception, or provide you with a rude or enlightening awakening. My favorite feedback experience was when I had the privilege of attending an executive leadership development program. Before the workshop, we were assaulted with homework and then spent the entire week all but battered with different kinds of feedback: assessment feedback, whole group feedback, small group feedback, individual feedback, and even a one-on-one session with an industrial psychologist. I became so paranoid about being judged that I was afraid to ask someone at dinner to pass the pepper out of fear that he might tell me I was too passive and should just grab it myself. To overcome this faux pas, I demonstrated my newfound assertiveness by providing some feedback to my boss in front of some co-workers, which wasn't an emotionally intelligent idea.

In any event, if you would like to explore some of these assessment tools please refer to the Recommended Resources list in the appendices for some assessment resources. Even if you don't choose this path, you can solicit some feedback just by asking those around you what they think of you, how they see you, what they think you are good at, and so on. I know that the truth can hurt, but so does transition. It's also a good kind of pain because it is most often followed by pleasure. Graciously receiving (and also providing) constructive feedback is an important life skill and can help you become more self-aware and emotionally intelligent.

Recipe: The Perfect Pancake

Mix values and strengths with
tools that can be learned:

cognitive reframing, mindfulness,
relaxation, visualization, emotional
intelligence, skills, and knowledge

Once you have made your perfect pancake, you're ready to
move on to the next stage, digestion.

Digestion

"You're alive. Do something. The directive in life, the
moral imperative was so uncomplicated. It could be
expressed in single words, not complete sentences.
It sounded like this. Look. Listen. Choose. Act."
—Barbara Hall

After a successful perfect pancake stage, some reach the
digestion stage, or acceptance. You probably have grown in a
cognitive, emotional, and/or spiritual way. By the way, those who
are still stuck in the blender stage may not get to this stage and
should seek professional help to get out of the blender. A more
elevated mood accompanies digestion, which is positive. My
prior life in financial services is so foreign to me now that it seems
surreal, as though the twenty-one years I spent in that sector were
just a fleeting dream. I have completely put the past behind me
and accepted the new status quo. I'm confident in your ability to
reach satiety by using the provided tools.

Larry, for example, worked for twenty-two years in the
lending business. He actually loved his work, particularly the
time he spent calling on clients and entertaining them. After the
bank eliminated his job, he spent his time in the blender stage
and then made his perfect pancake as a boat captain. He turned
his passions for being outside, being with others, and fishing into
a small business. He shed those itchy suits, and the only boards
he had room for were surfboards, wakeboards, and man-over-
boards. The idea of working in a corporate setting was so foreign
that he called it his "prior life."

Similarly, Suzanne had worked outside of her home in real estate for more than twenty-five years when she was diagnosed with Parkinson's disease. She had always worked but no longer felt comfortable around a lot of people. With the help of her supportive friends and family, she thought up a new home-based business idea. She started a housecleaning service and used some of her real estate clients to kick-start it. She hired some friends to call on clients and ran the business's other aspects from her home. After the first year, she had so fully digested her transition that she felt she could never go back. In fact, she really liked the fact that her boardroom was her bedroom.

The Plan

"Life is what happens to you while
you're busy making other plans."
—John Lennon

Once you have digested the vision for your new pancake, you now need to create a plan for how to act out your values, build on your strengths, and maximize your life satisfaction. This means identifying the steps you'll take to achieve your vision of your new life. Create a vision, make a plan, and take action. If three steps are too many for you, pick action because otherwise you might regress to immobilization and spend too much time thinking and too little time acting.

At this juncture, I feel that I should launch into a long dissertation on how to create your strategic life plan. I could wallpaper every room in my house and yours with all of the strategic business plans I created during my twenty-one years in banking. But I think I'll pass on the lecture and boil (or bake) the perfect pancake plan down to three steps: vision, strategy, and plan.

The vision is the big picture, or the what. For example, "I'm going to become a psychotherapist when my children are grown." The strategy is the how, the broad-brush way in which you are going to achieve your vision. For example, "I'm going to get my master's degree, do my internship, and gain the necessary skills and experience to become a psychotherapist." The plan comprises the action steps; it's the where-the-rubber-meets-the-road measures that you're taking to keep with your strategy and obtain your vision. For example, "I'm going to fill out the graduate school application; then, I'm going to register; then, I'm going to purchase my books."

When it comes to the plan or the goals, I can't stress enough that they need to be specific, attainable, and measurable. Don't set goals so high that not achieving them will lead to cognitive distortions, like labeling and overgeneralizing. Establish specific goals that are a stretch but can be achieved, and make sure that you can tell when you have achieved them. Although I have been advocating that you search for happiness, when it comes to goals, think SAD, **s**pecific, **a**ctionable, and **d**oable. For example:

- Take five deep abdominal breaths at least once each day.
- Exercise for thirty minutes five times a week.
- Reframe five thoughts a week.
- Relax for at least twenty minutes five times a week,
- Make a stack of five pancakes one morning a week.

Tell someone else about your goals so that you're accountable to another party and, thus, more likely to follow through. If you have someone to answer to, you are more likely to lose weight, quit smoking, or whatever else you resolve to do. Share your goals with your partner, a friend, your family, or your coach. And most important of all, make sure you act on those goals.

> "If we don't change direction soon,
> we'll end up where we're going."
> —Professor Irwin Corey

Regarding my own transition plan, I decided to go forward, and not back, by registering for the psychology program after my extracurricular stint in executive search work. My vision for my future was to leverage my strengths of making connections and building rapport in an empathic manner. I wanted to make a difference by helping clients make positive changes in their lives and work enough to satisfy my need for achievement while placing family first and health/recreation second. I was able to test-drive this plan during the internship phase of the program.

Recipe: SAD Goals

1. Specific

2. Actionable

3. Doable

"Knowledge must come through action; you can
have no test which is not fanciful, save by trial."
—Sophocles

I must tell you that the first few days on the job were surreal.
I actually had to glance down at my name-tag to make sure
that it really was me working with the clients in front of me.
I absolutely savored my time as an intern at the community
hospital. The personal rewards of this profession are so infinite
and almost impossible to articulate, while the financial rewards
are infinitesimal. (Why is that so often the case?)

As graduation approached, I think I regressed to denial
because I didn't initially sign up to attend the ceremony. About
a week before, I changed my mind. I remembered that when I
had started the degree program, my sons had asked me if I would
wear one of those goofy hats when I graduated. I felt that I kind
of owed it to them in return for all of the encouragement they
had provided me. (Besides, they got to leave school early for the
afternoon ceremony, which did wonders for my approval rating.)
My father, brothers, husband, and sons cheered me on, and I got
a very stiff neck from turning around to bask in their support.

Knowing how wonderful it was to be supported, I was anxious
to begin my new career, in which I could create a warm, accepting,
nonjudgmental, empathic environment to facilitate change and
growth for others. My new life chapter was to begin. Of course, I
mindfully savored a glass of champagne that evening to celebrate
with my family (maybe even another glass the next night thanks
to the kindness of friends who acted on my unsubtle hints about
my taste for the bubbly).

This time around, I was certain that my next step was a
no-brainer—that with a counseling psychology degree I would
become a counseling psychologist. In fact my degree and
internship opened up a whole new world of options. So I could
stay on the perfect pancake fence a while longer, I decided to

investigate a relatively new arena called personal and executive coaching. Coaching focuses on helping well-functioning individuals create a vision for their future and, more importantly, take action to achieve their goals and desires. The International Coach Federation, on its Web site, www.coachfederation. org, defines coaching as "partnering with clients in a thought-provoking and creative process that inspires them to maximize their personal and professional potential. Professional coaches provide an ongoing partnership designed to help clients produce fulfilling results in their personal and professional lives. Coaches help people improve their performance and enhance the quality of their lives. Coaches are trained to listen, to observe, and to customize their approach to individual client needs. They seek to elicit solutions and strategies from the client; they believe the client is naturally creative and resourceful. The coach's job is to provide support to enhance the skills, resources, and creativity that the client already has."

Achieving greater balance in your life, enhancing overall life satisfaction, developing greater professional competence, and managing transitions are examples of coaching goals. Psychotherapy is more about emotional healing and alleviating distress or impairment in your functioning. Learning better coping skills, processing troubling emotions, or changing ways of thinking and/or behaving are the domain of psychotherapy.

It occurred to me that I could leverage my business background, marry it with the psychology training, and provide personal and/or executive coaching services. It was kind of a combo (like pancakes and syrup) job idea that would incorporate my values, my strengths, my talents, and my skills and experience. I could retain the flexibility to enjoy family time, be able to help others, and put my life experience to work. I was still torn though because in my heart, I had experienced the rich rewards of providing psychotherapy in a community hospital setting. The question was again, "Tory, what do you want to be when you grow up?"

(Between us and off the record, I *didn't* want to grow up [or at least old], especially now that people were addressing me as "ma'am." In addition, I was having such a great time being around children. Adulthood actually is highly overrated unless you keep making pancakes as you go along by seeking out opportunities to grow, develop, and transition throughout life. And besides, I couldn't think of a flexible job schedule that would coincide exactly with my own children's schedules. I could just picture the position wanted ad: "Loves children; wants to work during the school day only; and have summers, weekends, and obscure holidays off." Can you think of a job like that [excluding academia of course]? In my head, I completely understood why my demands to work only on alternating Tuesdays when the moon was full were unreasonable. After all, I had been on the other side of the desk.

The answer had been right there in front of me all of these years. I just needed to act on the perfect pancake recipe and combine my strengths and values with the proper tools. My priceless value (family time) still topped the list, but my vision for the future included an eerily quiet house. I decided to leverage my strengths by becoming a psychotherapist, as well as a personal and executive coach. This way I could help people achieve greater life satisfaction whether they believe their functioning is impaired or not. And best of all, I could help people go through the blender stages without being completely crushed. And finally, of course, I also became a writer, so that I could help a wider audience to make better pancakes in kitchens far and wide.

I must confess that I feel very fortunate that the bank eliminated my position. Without that wake-up call, I might never have found the perfect pancake. It was not always fun in the blender stage; in fact, at times, it was downright depressing. I might have even sought the help of a therapist, and that experience might have inspired me to become one. Either way, I believe that I have found my calling, and I'm honored to help others find greater happiness. It's wonderful not to be an impostor any longer and to savor this delicious pancake.

> "Make the most of yourself, for
> that is all there is of you."
> —Ralph Waldo Emerson

Epilogue: The Last Pancake

Well, I certainly hope that you have enjoyed your journey through a sample life transition. Admittedly in some respects, my story is a how-not-to tale, (think frogs if you are struggling), but sometimes life's best lessons are those learned by trial and error along the way. I hope that during your transition times, the five-stage pancake model (the wake-up call, the first pancake, the blender, the perfect pancake, and digestion stages) at least provides you with some comfort that you haven't lost your mind but are in transition. And, of course, again I beg you to never lose your sense of humor, particularly about yourself. And I encourage you to use the transition survival tools, which I've offered to you: cognitive behavioral therapy, mindfulness, relaxation, visualization, emotional intelligence, exercise, cinematherapy, bibliotherapy, laughter, and *practice*. In summary, I'd like to leave you with ten quotations relevant to transition, since after all:

"I love quotations because it is a joy to find thoughts
one might have, beautifully expressed with much
authority by someone recognized wiser than oneself."
—Marlene Dietrich

Tory's Top Ten Transition Themes

- "You must be the change you want to see in the world." —Mahatma Ghandi
- "I believe that life is a journey, often difficult and sometimes incredibly cruel, but we are well equipped for it only if we tap into our talents and gifts and allow them to blossom." —Les Brown
- "If a man insisted always on being serious and never allowed himself a bit of fun and relaxation, he would go mad." —Herodotus
- "If you can attain repose and calm, believe that you have seized happiness." —Julie-Jeanne-Eleonore de Lespinasse
- "The unexamined life is not worth living." —Socrates
- "Life's too short, so love the one you got. 'Cause you might get run over or you might get shot." —Sublime
- "Knowledge is power." —Sir Francis Bacon
- "Happiness depends on ourselves." —Aristotle
- "Change your thoughts, and you change your world." —Norman Vincent Peale
- "Pride is the recognition of the fact that you are your own highest value, and like all of man's values, it has to be earned." —Ayn Rand
- "Without the first pancake, there would be no second." —Tory Wilcox

And finally (promise); *yes*, I know that was more than "ten"; I just wanted to ensure that you were reading mindfully. If not turn back to page one, take two Advil, and call me in the morning.

Real Pancake Tips

I don't want to disappoint those of you who thought this book would literally help you make better pancakes, and so I close with the following suggestions:

- It's all about the griddle heat. For regular-weight batters (like buttermilk), the grill temperature should be 375 to 380 degrees, but for heavier batters (like buckwheat), go about ten degrees cooler. If the heat isn't just right, you can end up with overcooked outsides and undercooked centers.
- The best way to gauge the temperature is to do a couple of test pancakes. Be prepared to discard them and move on (sound familiar?).
- For a regular-sized cake, use about one-fourth to one-third cup of batter and pour it about three inches above the griddle.
- Once the dry-edged bubbles begin to appear on the pancake, check if the underside is golden brown. If so, it's time to flip.
- Once both sides are honey colored, the pancake is ready. (Remember, stacking the pancakes can make them soggy from sweating and putting them in the oven can dry them out.)
- Apply butter and syrup. Grab a fork and knife, and *enjoy*.

Recommended Resources

Cognitive Behavioral Therapy

- Burns, David D. *The Feeling Good Handbook.* New York: Plume/Penguin Putnam, 1999.
- Burns, David D. *Ten Days to Self-Esteem.* New York: Harper Collins, 1993.
- Beck, Aaron T. et al. *Cognitive Therapy for Depression.* New York: Guilford Press, 1987.
- McKay, Matthew et al. *Thoughts and Feeling: Taking Control of Your Moods.* Oakland, California: New Harbinger Publications, 1997.
- Wilson, Rob and Rhena Branch. *Cognitive Behavioral Therapy for Dummies,* London: John Wiley and Sons, 2006.

Bibliotherapy

- Levinson, Daniel. *Seasons of a Man's Life,* New York: Ballantine Books, 1986.
- Levinson, Daniel. *Seasons of a Woman's Life,* New York: Ballantine Books, 1997.
- Spencer, Sabrina, and John Adams. *Life Changes: A Guide to the Seven Stages of Personal Growth,.* New York, Paraview Press, 2002..
- Bridges, William. *The Way of Transition: Embracing Life's Most Difficult Moments.* Cambridge, Massachusetts: Perseus Publishing, 2001.
- Buffone, Gary. *The Myth of Tomorrow: Seven Essential Keys for Living the Life You Want.* New York: McGraw-Hill, 2002.
- Johnson, Spencer, MD. *Who Moved My Cheese?* New York: G.P. Putnam and Sons, 2002.
- Richardson, Cheryl. *Take Time for Your Life.* New York: Broadway Books, 1998.

Cinematherapy

- Peske, Nancy, and Beverly West. *Cinematherapy for the Soul: The Girl's Guide to Finding Inspiration One Movie At A Time.* New York, Dell Trade Paperback.. (See also numerous other topical books by the same author.)
- Solomon, Gary. *Reel Therapy: How Movies Inspire You to Overcome Life's Problems.* New York: Lebhar-Friedman Books, 2001.
- Solomon, Gary. *The Motion Picture Prescription: Watch This Movie and Call Me in the Morning: 200 Movies to Help You Heal Life's Problems.* Publisher's City: Asian Pub, 1995.
- www.cinematherapy.com: Using Movies for Healing and Growth.
- www.rogerebert.suntimes.com

Mindfulness

- Kabat-Zinn, Jon. *Coming to Our Senses: Healing Ourselves and the World Through Mindfulness.* New York: Hyperion Press, 2006. (See other topical books by the same author including the one below.)
- Brantley, Jeffrey. *Calming Your Anxious Mind: How Mindfulness and Compassion Can Free You from Anxiety, Fear, and Panic.* Oakland, California: New Harbinger Publications, Inc., 2003.
- Kabat-Zinn, Jon. *Wherever You Go, There You Are: Mindfulness Meditation in Everyday Life.* New York: Hyperion Press, 1994.
- Mindfulness meditation tapes with Jon Kabat-Zinn. http://www.mindfulnesstapes.com/index.html.

Relaxation and Self-Care

- Davis, Martha, Eshelman, Elizabeth, and Matthew McKay. *The Relaxation and Stress Reduction Workbook.* Oakland, California: New Harbinger Publications, Inc., 2000.
- Kabat-Zinn, Jon, et al. *Full Catastrophe Living: Using the Wisdom of Your Body and Mind to Face Stress, Pain, and Illness.* New York: Dell Publishing, 1990.

- Benson, Herbert, and Miriam Klipper. *The Relaxation Response.* New York: Harper Collins, 2000.

Emotional Intelligence

- Goleman, Daniel. *Emotional Intelligence: Why It Can Matter More Than IQ.* 10th anniversary ed. New York: Bantam Books, 2006.
- Goleman, Daniel. *Social Intelligence: The New Science of Human Relationships.* New York: Random House, 2007.
- Segal, Jeanne S. *Raising Your Emotional Intelligence: A Practical Guide.* New York: Henry Holt, 1997.

Assessment Instruments

- www.authentichappiness.com contains a variety of assessments including the Satisfaction with Life Scale included in chapter 3.
- *Myers-Briggs Type Indicator (MBTI):* This costs money and requires the interpretive assistance of a certified MBTI practitioner (or see www.myersbriggs.org).
- *Jung-Myers Briggs Typology Test:* This test is free and self-directed and can be taken online at www.humanmetrics.com. It gives you a four-letter personality type indicator and an explanation of the results. You can purchase a ten-page report for more personal analysis.
- Rath, T., *StrengthsFinder2.0: A New and Upgraded Edition.* New York: Gallup Press, 2007.
- Simon, S. *In Search of Values: 31 Strategies for Finding out What Really Matters Most to You.* New York: Warner Books, 1993.
- *Self-Directed Search:* This is a fee-based online assessment that takes only fifteen to twenty minutes to complete and helps match careers and educational pursuits with your own skills and interests (www.self-directedsearch.com).
- Bolles, Richard Nelson. *What Color Is Your Parachute? 2008: A Practical Manual for Job- Hunters and Career- Changers.* Berkeley, California: Ten Speed Press, 2008. This book has been around since the parachute was invented and has been

completely revised. It remains one of the most highly regarded resources for job seeking or just self-assessment.

Women's Topics

- Anything and everything on the Lifetime Channel
- Markoff, Heidi, et al. *What to Expect When You Are Expecting.* 3rd ed. New York: Workman Publishing Company, 2002.
- Eisenberg, Arlene, et al. *What to Expect the First Year.* New York: Workman Publishing Company, 2004.
- Ferrare, Christina. *Okay, So I Don't Have a Headache.* New York: St. Martin' s Press, 1999.
- Northrup, Christine. *The Wisdom of Menopause: Creating Physical and Emotional Health and Healing During the Change.* New York: Bantam Dell, 2006.
- www.menopausethemusical.com

References

American Psychiatric Association. *Diagnostic and Statistical Manual of Mental Disorders (DSM-IV-TR)*. 4th ed. Washington, DC: American Psychiatric Association, 2000.

Beck, Aaron T., A. John Rush, Brian F. Shaw, and Gary Emery. *Cognitive Therapy of Depression*. New York: Guilford Press, 1979.

Benson, Herbert. *The Relaxation Response*. 2nd ed. New York: Harper Collins, 2000.

Buckingham, Marcus, and Donald O. Clifton. *Now, Discover Your Strengths*. New York: Free Press, 2001.

Buffone, Gary. *The Myth of Tomorrow: Seven Essential Keys for Living the Life You Want*. New York: McGraw-Hill, 2002.

Burns, David D. *The Feeling Good Handbook*. New York: Plume/Penguin Putnam, 1999.

Davis, Martha, Elizabeth Robbins Eshelman, and Matthew McKay. *The Relaxation and Stress Reduction Workbook*. 5th ed. Oakland, California: New Harbinger Publications, 2000.

Diener, Ed, Robert A. Emmons, Randy J. Larsen, and Sharon Griffin. 1985. The satisfaction with life scale. *Journal of Personality Assessment* Vol. 49, No. 1.

Ellis, Albert, and Catharine MacLaren. *Rational Emotive Behavior Therapy: A Therapist's Guide*. 2nd ed. Atascadero, California: Impact Publishers, 1998.

Erikson, Erik H. *Identity: Youth and Crisis*. New York: W.W. Norton, 1968.

Gardner, Howard. *Frames of Mind: The Theory of Multiple Intelligences*. New York, NY: Perseus Books, 1993.

Goleman, Daniel. *Emotional Intelligence: Why It Can Matter More Than IQ*. New York: Bantam Books, 1997.

Hudson, Frederic M. *The Handbook of Coaching: A Comprehensive Resource Guide for Managers, Executives, Consultants, and Human Resource Professionals*. New York: Jossey-Bass, 1999.

Jacobson, Edmund. *Progressive Relaxation: A Physiological and Clinical Investigation of Muscular States and Their Significance in Psychology and Medical Practice.* 3rd ed. Chicago: University of Chicago Press, 1974.

Kabat-Zinn, Jon. *Wherever You Go, There You Are: Mindfulness Meditation in Everyday Life.* New York: Hyperion, 1994.

Kübler-Ross, Elisabeth, and David Kessler. *On Grief and Grieving: Finding the Meaning of Grief Through the Five Stages of Grieving.* New York: Scribner, 2005.

Levinson, Daniel J. *The Seasons of a Man's Life.* New York: Ballantine Books, 1978.

Piaget, Jean, and Bärbel Inhelder. *The Psychology of the Child.* 2nd ed. New York: Basic Books, 2000.

Rosemond, John. *The New Six-Point Plan for Raising Happy, Healthy Children.* Kansas City, Missouri: Andrew McMeel Publishing, LLC, 2006.

Spencer, Sabina A., and John D. Adams. *Life Changes: A Guide to the Seven Stages of Personal Growth.* New York: Paraview Press, 2002.

Super, Donald. *Career, Education, and the Meanings of Work.* Washington DC: U.S. Office of Education, 1976.

Printed in the United States
132755LV00006B/53/P